- **Common and preferred stocks** • **Corporate and municipal bonds** • **Life insurance** • **Annuities** • **Collectibles** • **Ginnie Maes** • **CDs** • **Unit trusts** • **Options and futures** • **Real estate investments**

From "lending" investments to "owning" investments, from high-risk trading strategies to fixed-income investments, whether you're just starting out or planning your retirement, *The Morgan Stanley Guide to Personal Investing* puts your financial future where it should be—in your own hands. It is the essential tool for making your money work for you . . . today and tomorrow.

"Writing in a comfortable, low-key tone, Gardiner explains complex concepts with lively examples and humorous quotes and anecdotes . . . A solid overview."
—*Booklist*

ROBERT M. GARDINER, former chairman and CEO of Dean Witter Financial Services Group, continues as a senior advisor to Morgan Stanley Dean Witter & Co. He has also served as chairman of the National Association of Securities Dealers, vice-chairman of the New York Stock Exchange, and founding chairman of the Securities Industry Association. He lives in New Jersey and Florida.

Morgan Stanley is a service mark of Morgan Stanley Dean Witter & Co. Services are offered through Morgan Stanley DW Inc., member SIPC.

THE
MORGAN STANLEY

GUIDE TO

PERSONAL

INVESTING

REVISED EDITION

ROBERT M. GARDINER

A DUTTON BOOK

PUBLISHER'S NOTE
This publication is designed to provide accurate and authoritative information with regard to the subject matter covered. It is sold with the understanding that the publisher is not engaged in rendering financial, accounting, or other professional services. If financial advice or other expert assistance is required, the services of a competent professional should be sought.

DUTTON
Published by the Penguin Group
Penguin Books USA Inc., 375 Hudson Street,
New York, New York 10014, U.S.A.
Penguin Books Ltd, 27 Wrights Lane,
London W8 5TZ, England
Penguin Books Australia Ltd, Ringwood,
Victoria, Australia
Penguin Books Canada Ltd, 10 Alcorn Avenue,
Toronto, Ontario, Canada M4V 3B2
Penguin Books (N.Z.) Ltd, 182–190 Wairau Road,
Auckland 10, New Zealand

Penguin Books Ltd, Registered Offices:
Harmondsworth, Middlesex, England

This revised edition first published by Dutton, an imprint of Dutton Signet,
a division of Penguin Books USA Inc.
Distributed in Canada by McClelland & Stewart Inc..

First Printing, July 1997
First Printing (Revised Special Sales Edition), June 2001
10 9 8 7 6 5 4 3 2 1

Copyright © Dean Witter Financial Services, Inc., 1988
Copyright © Dean Witter Discover & Co., 1997
Copyright © Morgan Stanley Dean Witter & Co., 1998, 2001
All rights reserved

 REGISTERED TRADEMARK—MARCA REGISTRADA

LIBRARY OF CONGRESS CATALOGING-IN-PUBLICATION DATA:
Gardiner, Robert M.
   The Morgan Stanley guide to personal investing / Robert M. Gardiner.—Rev. ed.
   p.   cm.
   Includes index.
   ISBN 0-525-94522-9 (acid-free paper)
   1. Investments—Handbooks, manuals, etc.   I. Title.
HG4527.G37   1997
332.67'8—dc21   97-4956
                                                                    CIP

Printed in the United States of America
Set in New Baskerville
Designed by Leonard Telesca

This book is printed on acid-free paper. ∞

ACKNOWLEDGMENTS

Preparing the revised edition of this book has been a collaborative process involving many people throughout Morgan Stanley, and I am pleased to acknowledge their assistance.

The person who coordinated the entire effort and who made sure deadlines were met was Kathy McIntee, and I am deeply indebted to her.

Many Morgan Stanley investment professionals gave generously of their time in helping me assess the new investment landscape. They provided information and valuable insights about their respective areas, and I would like to thank the following for their contributions:

Liz McCarthy and Art Bradley, equities; Terry Fuller and Linda Ward, insurance; Rosalie Clough and Jack Kemp, mutual funds; Mark Holtzer, credit services; Kara Valentine, financial planning; Sandy Motusesky and Glenn Tom, online services; Larry Schneider and Allison Johnson, futures; John Gross, tax issues; Maryanne Elias, Individual Retirement Accounts; Ian Bernstein, fixed income securities; Claude Czekaj, unit trusts; Scott Witherspoon, lending services; and Christine Diehl and Cathy Weigel, other editorial support.

Additionally, I would like to thank Michael Gregg, a senior attorney at Morgan Stanley, who dealt with the legal matters associated with publishing a book, and Louise Otten-Kacerek, who handled the many necessary administrative tasks.

I am also indebted to my agent, Amanda Urban at ICM, for her assistance in bridging the gap between Wall Street and Publisher's Row. And I would like to thank our editors at Penguin Putnam for facilitating the development of this revised edition.

Finally, I want to thank the many individuals within and outside of Morgan Stanley whose positive comments about the previous editions provided the encouragement that spurred the effort. I hope they will find the revised edition a useful guide in their efforts to achieve financial serenity.

CONTENTS

PREFACE

On April 1, 1946, I began my career in the securities business. The stock market at that time was in the midst of a post–World War II rally. The Dow Jones Industrial Average hit the then-dizzying peak of 212.50. All was wine and roses.

And then the market collapsed. Before the year was over, the Dow fell to 163. Wall Street was overtaken by gloom.

The gloom lasted for a long time. The market didn't reach its 1946 peak again until 1950. But during those down years, as young and green as I was, I knew one thing: There were bargains to be had. In fact, you could have picked them with your eyes closed. All you had to do was select from a list of quality companies—and wait. They would go up again.

And they did. The market boomed through most of the 1950s—as it has boomed following every slump in history (and slumped following every boom). This is what some people forgot following the bear market of 1973–74 and the market "meltdown" of October 1987: The market goes up and the market goes down—but in the long run, it goes up. Some fifty years after I entered the securities business, the Dow Jones Industrial Average crossed 7000 to reach an all-time record.

And as the greatest bull market of the century continued, by 1999 the Dow soared to over 10,000. With the new millennium came more unprecedented territory for the Dow, which crossed 11,000.

The run-up in the Nasdaq Composite in recent years has been even more remarkable, as shares of high-tech companies, which are a major part of that index, advanced dramatically in the 1990s. From 752 at year-end 1994, the Nasdaq Composite breached the 5000 level in the spring of 2000 before a much-needed correction brought the index back to around 4000 at midyear.

When I started on Wall Street, trading volume for the year was less than an average day's trading in 1996. In August 1967, the New York Stock Exchange started closing at 2:00 P.M. and then shut down on Wednesday because the back office couldn't keep up with the trading volume—13 million shares a day. By 2000, average trading volume on the NYSE was more than one billion shares per day, and billion share days have become commonplace on Nasdaq as well.

Back in 1946, not too many Americans were worried about the stock market, because only a handful of people owned shares of stock.

Brokerage houses were not oriented toward, or even interested in, individual investors of modest means. Stock exchange rules required brokers with ground-floor offices to paint their windows black. They needed special permission to put up displays. Drop-in customers were clearly not expected—or invited.

The stock market was dominated by wealthy individuals and large institutions. Individuals who were less than rich were also shut out from other types of investment opportunities that were available to their millionaire cousins. There were no giant pension plans investing money on behalf of thousands of workers. There weren't any money market accounts, no central asset accounts, no 401(k) plans or individual retirement accounts. When it came to life insurance, the small number of Americans who wanted more than burial insurance had their choice of whole life or term, take it or leave it. Mutual funds were available for only a limited variety of investment instruments and objectives.

Until the 1960s, unless you were fairly rich you probably kept most of your money in a low-interest savings account and a no-interest checking account. There wasn't much else you could do with it.

Then came the high-inflation years of the late 1970s. People learned very quickly that keeping their money in fixed-interest savings accounts was a sure way to lose ground. Their savings grew so slowly that they were actually *losing* money even while they saved. So they began to look for ways to make their money work harder.

Their search coincided with a wave of deregulation in the financial services industry. Gaps were broken in the artificial barriers separating banks, savings and loan associations, securities brokers, and insurance companies. The more aggressive of those institutions took advantage of the opportunities to compete for investors' dollars by offering new, higher-yielding investment vehicles. Within a few years, the landscape of American investments had changed forever. There are now scores of ways—and places—for individuals and families to put their money to work at attractive rates of return.

Among those coming face-to-face with this profusion of choices today are millions of new investors. They include members of the baby boom generation now reaching their peak earning years. Or they are recent retirees, now taking personal control of pension dollars previously managed by pension funds. They include individuals who have built up substantial nest eggs in their 401(k) plans and are now ready to place that money in higher-yielding investments than the guaranteed investment contracts that they often began with.

These new investors are more sophisticated than the new investors of years past. Many of them have been forced to gain some experience in the financial world because of their 401(k) plans. Many have had their appetite for investing whetted by the proliferation of sources of investment information. Before the 1990s, there were no *Smart Money* or *Worth* magazines writing about investments for a general audience. Nor was there a CNBC broadcasting financial news around the clock. Many of the newcomers to investing have a high degree of self-reliance; they know they don't want to be dependent on Social Security in their retirement years. They're prepared to compare alternative investment vehicles and to choose among them rationally.

Many have chosen the stock market. The number of individuals owning shares in American corporations has climbed from 25 million in 1975 to nearly 80 million in 2000. Others have chosen to invest in some of the new instruments that didn't even exist a decade ago. Still others, however, are trying to decide among the bewildering array of choices available to them.

Here at Morgan Stanley, I believe we have done more than any other brokerage firm in America to help new investors make their choices. As I look around at all the financial services companies that target the affluent few, I am reminded of the guru who said, "So many religions look after the poor. Leave the rich to me." We have always followed a different path than many of our competitors. When Dean Witter founded his firm in 1924, it was dedicated to serving the financial needs of individual investors. This was a guiding principle of Mr. Dean Witter himself, who once declared, "In the long run those firms which survive and prosper are those who maintain conservative policies and put their customers' interests first."

Historically, Dean Witter was always a conservative firm. During the Great Depression, when many other securities firms struggled and some disappeared, Dean Witter made a profit every year because it refrained from imprudent speculation during the feverish boom that preceded the Great Crash. Morgan Stanley, a descendant of the J.P. Morgan banking house, was also a model of financial stability. Morgan Stanley and Dean Witter merged in 1997, and our brand name is now Morgan Stanley. Today, Morgan Stanley offers investments that are secure enough for even our most cautious clients yet offer competitive rates of return. Clients with a higher tolerance for risk—and only those clients—have their choice of investments offering the prospect of very high rates of return. The firm now offers an array of investments that cover the spectrum in terms of risks and returns. But it is in the best interests of the Morgan Stanley financial advisor to preserve his or her client's capital. Our financial advisors are not compensated only by buying and selling securities. They are also rewarded for growth in their clients' accounts, mutual fund holdings, and other steady accumulations of clients' wealth.

I entered the securities business as a research analyst at A. M. Kidder & Company, and I worked my way up to become chairman of Reynolds Securities in 1978, when the firm merged with Dean Witter. Three years later, Dean Witter Reynolds was acquired by Sears, Roebuck and Co. In 1986, we launched the Discover Card to meet the credit card needs of individual consumers. In 1993, Dean Witter and the Discover Card were spun off by Sears, and we once again became an independent, publicly owned company. And then, in 1997, Dean Witter, Discover & Co. and Morgan Stanley Group Inc. merged, forming Morgan Stanley Dean Witter & Co., the world's largest securities firm.

Thus, I have not only closely watched the stock market as an investor and a brokerage firm executive, I have also experienced the market from the perspective of an executive at a publicly held company that has issued stocks and bonds. My years in the brokerage business have given me good feelings about stocks, despite the ups and downs of the market. (I explain why in Chapter 6.) I believe that investors of even modest means can do well for themselves in stocks. I've seen many of them do so.

But there's a whole world of other investments out there, a world that keeps expanding rapidly. Many of these investments have their own distinct advantages and risks. I have drawn on the knowledge and experience of colleagues throughout Morgan Stanley to include them in this book.

We have no ax to grind. Morgan Stanley offers almost every type of investment available anywhere, from money market

funds to municipal bonds to gold coins. Our view is simply
that all of our clients—and potential clients—are better off
with some type of investment or savings program.

This book is offered in the hope it will guide you toward
the investment program that's best for you.

THE
MORGAN STANLEY
GUIDE TO
PERSONAL
INVESTING

CHAPTER 1

THE SLOW ROAD

TO RICHES

Drifting Along

Many people drift along from paycheck to paycheck. They take care of their bills and put gas in the car. When they have a few extra dollars, they go out to dinner and catch a movie.

They have a savings account, but also a mortgage and some credit card bills. They know they're covered by Social Security—although a growing number of younger Americans doubt whether they'll ever collect anything from it. They're probably also covered by some kind of employer-sponsored pension or profit-sharing plan, but they generally haven't thought too much about how it works or how to make the most of it. They earn their money, they spend it to live, and life goes on.

Still, in the backs of their minds, they know they should be devoting some serious thought to their financial affairs. How will they send the kids to college? What will they live on in their old age? How should they invest the money in their 401(k) plan? How can they select the right investments from the whole gamut of new financial products and services that have been created in the past twenty years? What's the story on those zero coupon bonds, mortgage-backed securities, real estate investment trusts, variable annuities, Roth IRAs, and all of those thousands of mutual funds? It takes time to learn about these things, and most people don't have much extra time. So the weeks go by, and then the years, and people live their lives with a vague but constant worry that someday, they're not going to have enough money.

It doesn't have to be this way. Anyone who can earn a decent living and knows how to add, multiply, and divide (or, failing that, how to work a calculator) can do a whole lot better than just get by. People with unexceptional incomes can, without great hardship, make arrangements to guarantee their future financial security. They can, in fact, accumulate small fortunes. There's nothing magical about the process. It doesn't require great luck or great skill. It does, however, require financial planning and discipline. And it requires you to abandon the idea that you can get rich quick. You can't. What you can do, however, if you work at it, is get rich slowly. Wouldn't you be foolish not to try?

There Is No Santa Claus

A stockbroker I know, when he was just starting out, kept a neat little notebook full of information about his clients and prospects, just as beginning stockbrokers are supposed to. Whenever he met with a new client, he would take out his notebook and dutifully ask, "Why do you want to invest?"

"To make money," the client would reply, and he would look at the broker doubtfully. Why on earth did this joker think he wanted to invest? To while away the lazy afternoons?

"That's fine," said the broker, and he would write "to make money" on the appropriate line in his notebook. (Pretty soon he had an entire notebook filled with clients whose investment goals were "to make money.")

The broker's next question was, "How much money do you want to make?"

The clients' answers varied, but they rarely put any limit on how much they wanted to make. What their answers boiled down to was, "All the money in the world."

"Well," the broker would say, "would you by any chance settle for $100 million?" The broker soon realized that his clients didn't really want all the money in the world, and they didn't even really want $100 million. What they wanted, in fact, was no specific amount of money at all. What they wanted was a feeling.

I call that feeling "financial serenity."

Financial serenity is a state of mind. It comes over people when they have achieved a standard of living that they're comfortable with, and have enough money to maintain that standard of living for the rest of their lives. Things might get even better, but that's not the point. The most important point is that things are never going to get worse.

Financial serenity is really another way of describing financial independence. It means that a person has enough money set aside and working for her that she doesn't have to rely on any financial source beyond her control. She doesn't have to fear a recession or a business downturn. She doesn't have to pray that little Jerome, who never was too good at math, will receive a college scholarship. He doesn't have to work after retirement if he doesn't want to. He doesn't have to rely entirely on Social Security or any other government program or family help to provide him with a respectable living in his old age.

You can achieve financial independence if you want to. You can enjoy the cozy feeling of financial serenity, a state in which those nagging little doubts about the future are forever banished. If you don't achieve financial security, it will be for a very simple reason: You didn't plan.

You wouldn't be alone in that. Fewer than half of all people age 20 or over have written financial plans.* Instead, they develop elaborate rationalizations for why they aren't planning for their financial futures. They blame their parents,

*Source: 1999 Consumer Survey, Certified Financial Planners Board of Standards.

who failed to leave them an inheritance. They insist that the little guy doesn't have a chance in the financial markets, so why bother. Or they procrastinate, promising that next week, next year, after the next raise, they will begin to put a little something away.

Or, sometimes, they try one thing. They buy a stock they hear about from Uncle Fred, or they take a flier in the commodities market. But the stock goes down ("You didn't actually buy that stock, did you?" says Uncle Fred), and they give up in dismay. Or they turn on their computer one day and buy some shares of stock on-line. And a little later, they sell those shares and buy some others based on what they read in some "chat room." That isn't really investing. That's gambling. That's looking for lightning to strike. That's following a rainbow.

I have some very sad news for these people, and it may be sad news for you too. I know many very intelligent people who have a hard time accepting it. Or they say they accept it, but they still handle their finances as if they'd never heard it.

This is the bad news: There is no Santa Claus.

This is a fact that most people learned with shock and sorrow when they were five years old. Yet it never ceases to amaze me how many intelligent, tough-minded, successful people believe in Santa Claus in their approach to investing.

Well, forget it. There really is no Santa Claus. Write that down and stick it on your refrigerator door. If a deal looks too good to be true, it is. If someone tells you that you can make a thousand dollars a week stuffing envelopes at home or stockpiling selenium in your basement, he's exaggerating. If Uncle Fred gives you some hot news about a stock that's sure to go up, ask yourself, "Why am I one of the few people in the entire United States of America privileged to hear this news? Why do I know something that many brilliant people who spend their entire lives studying the investment scene do not know?" The answer is, you don't. By the time you hear any hot news, it is cold, and it is already reflected in the price of the stock. (If you actually did have access to wonderful information, you would already be rich and you wouldn't be reading this book. If you're reading this book anyway, give me a call. Let's have lunch.)

The Impossible Quest

Even without the dubious advantage of allegedly hot news, many people go into the investment arena looking for $10 investments that will go to $15 in six months. They may never actually define their goal to themselves that way, but that's what it amounts to. They assume they are being quite reasonable and undemanding to set as a standard something like finding a $10 stock that will go to $15 in six months. After all, that calls for upward movement of less than one point a month. Shouldn't a reasonably astute selection be able to provide this?

No.

What such people are seeking, put another way, is a 50 percent return on their investment every six months. If you found such a stock (at $10 a share) and put $10,000 into it, you would be able to sell it six months later (at $15 a share) for $15,000. If you promptly reinvested that in another $10 stock that went to $15 in six months, you could sell that out for $22,500. A very nice profit for a year's work.

Reinvest that in another $10 stock that goes to $15, and then do it again, and at the end of the second year you would have $50,625. At the end of the third year, you would have $113,906. After six years, you would be a millionaire. After fifteen years, you would be a billionaire.

In less than another decade, you would be a trillionaire. And in another three or four years, you would own all the wealth on earth. Congratulations.

Do you still think it is reasonable to look for $10 stocks that will go to $15 in six months? Of course, you might find one once in a while. You may even find a couple. But you can't find them all the time, and you can't necessarily find one when you really need it. If you could consistently spot $10 stocks that went to $15—not in six months but in a year even—the world would beat a path to your door and people would be pleading with you to manage their investments for them.

Once you have accepted that there is no Santa Claus and developed reasonable expectations about investment returns, you are ready for financial planning and the serenity it can foster.

The Power of Compound Interest

You may have noticed something interesting about the growth of that $10,000 stake to a sum greater than the wealth of the world. In the first few years, the amount of money involved grew at a substantial but not unimaginable rate. Then it began to soar. This is an example of compound interest in action. That $10,000 was growing at an annual rate of 100 percent, compounded twice a year. That is, interest was paid on the original principal (the $10,000), and thereafter interest was paid on the principal and the accumulated interest as well.

The same thing happens in your savings account, although not quite so dramatically. If you have $1,000 in a bank that pays 5 percent interest, and that interest is compounded once a year, at the end of one year you will have $1,050 (your original $1,000 plus $50 interest). At the end of the second year, you will have not just $1,100 ($1,050 plus another $50 interest); you will have $1,102.50. You will have received interest on your original $1,000 and also on the interest you accumulated during the first year.

After three years, your $1,000 will grow to $1,160 (rounding off to the nearest dollar). After five years, you will have $1,280. After ten years, $1,630. Twenty years, $2,650. Thirty years, $4,320.

Not bad, but what if you could earn 10 percent on your money? After one year, you would have $1,100 instead of $1,050. Not much difference. After twenty years, however, instead of $2,650 you would have $6,730. After thirty years, instead of $4,320 you would have $17,450. All from an initial investment of $1,000. A few percentage points up or down in rate of return, over time, makes all the difference in the world.

There is no way you are going to earn a steady 100 percent on any investment (by finding $10 stocks that go to $15 in six months), but there is no reason to settle for 5 percent either. Somewhere between the interest rate your bank will pay you and the interest rate Santa Claus would happily pay you if he existed, there is a very nice rate of return that you can reasonably expect to earn in a well-conceived investment program. It is not at all far-fetched, for example, to look for—and find—$20 stocks that go to $21 or $22 in a year and pay a $1 dividend. Nor is it particularly difficult to earn a better return than you can get on your bank account by investing in bonds.

If you got a 10 percent return—5 percent from the dividend on a stock and 5 percent from the capital appreciation or increase in the price of the stock—that 10 percent can do nice things for you. If, starting at the age of thirty, you put $150 a month into an investment program that earns a steady 10 percent, at age sixty-five you will have $574,242. No tricks. No mirrors. You set aside some money. It grows. And then the growth grows. In 1748, Benjamin Franklin, who was a big fan of compound interest, described it like this: "Money is of a prolific, generating nature. Money can beget money, and its offspring can beget more."

Investing vs. Playing the Lottery

State lotteries have become popular in the United States. The prize is often $1 million. But sometimes the jackpot goes up to $60 or $80 million, and there are lines out the door at candy stores and newsstands that sell the lottery tickets. Millions of Americans plunk down a dollar or two every week, week after week, dreaming of winning the big prize.

The million-dollar prize, however, really doesn't amount to $1 million. If you read the fine print, lottery officials don't hand the winners $1 million checks. They hand them checks for $50,000 and promise to hand them another $50,000 every year for twenty years. Twenty times $50,000 does equal $1 million, but getting $50,000 each year for twenty years is a far different thing, and worth far less, than getting $1 million in a lump sum.

If lottery officials were to invest $500,000 at a 10 percent annual return, they would have $50,000 every year to give to a million-dollar winner, and at the end of twenty years, they would still have their $500,000. If they didn't care about getting their money back at the end, they could give away part of the principal every year along with the interest, working things out so that on the day the last check was due, there remained exactly $50,000 in the investment fund. To set up such a fund at 10 percent interest would cost $425,700. That, not $1 million, is what it costs a state lottery to give away a "million-dollar" prize.

If you had $425,700, you could set up your own fund and give yourself a check for $50,000 a year for twenty years. In fact, with a nest egg of that size, you might be able to provide yourself with checks for $50,000 for your whole life. And as I indicated, you can have $425,700 if you want to. Putting aside $150 a month from ages thirty to sixty-five at a 10 percent annual after-tax return will produce a fund of $574,242, which would put you in a better position than somebody who'd won a million-dollar lottery. If you put aside only $111 a month, at age 65, you can have $425,700, the exact equivalent of winning a million-dollar lottery at that age.

By the way, if you were to put just $2 a week into an investment program instead of using it to buy lottery tickets, at age sixty-five you would have $33,349. You could then start drawing out $64 a week for the rest of your life without ever touching the principal. This isn't quite a million dollars, but you don't need to have six Ping-Pong balls with your numbers on them come up in order to win this game. And there doesn't have to be a Santa Claus to give it to you. All that's required is a human being—you—undertaking a little financial planning and taking sensible steps to start off on the road to financial serenity.

CHAPTER 2

GETTING STARTED

Your Current Investment Program

Okay, you say, the idea of starting an investment program and having a financial plan sounds just fine. But at the moment, "I'm a little strapped for cash." Or, "I've got too much going on right now to take the time to figure out exactly what to do." Or, "I'm not sure I'm ready to start an investment program quite yet." So for a while anyway, "I'm not going to do a thing."

That's where you're wrong. You're already doing something. Doing nothing is doing something. Doing nothing means you've decided that the way you're handling your money right now is the way you will continue to handle your money.

And you are handling money, probably quite a bit of it. If you're in your early twenties and earning $35,000 a year, and if you expect to earn at least that much for the rest of your working life, over the next forty years, your lifetime income will be more than $1.4 million. Well over a million dollars will pass through your hands, and you're going to have to manage it somehow. Actually, you already have an investment program. You may not call it that, but it's there. Part of your

income is going to Social Security. You may be contributing
to a 401(k) plan or a payroll savings plan at work. You're presumably paying an insurance premium. You may be making
mortgage payments. You probably have some money in a
bank account. This is an investment program. It's probably
not the one you would choose if you sat down and looked at
all the alternatives, but you have chosen it, by default. On the
road to your financial future, you've decided to leave the map
at home.

Every day that you do nothing to rearrange your finances,
you are implicitly saying, "There is nothing I can do to improve my financial position." This is almost certainly not true.
You might, for example, have a substantial sum in a savings
account paying 5 percent interest, or in a checking account
paying no interest at all. You have it there because you regard
it as convenient and safe. You can easily get to it to cover both
regular expenses and possible emergencies. But, as we saw
during the high-inflation era of the late 1970s, the purchasing
power of money in bank accounts can actually dwindle away.
A dollar in a 5 percent savings account during a period of
10 percent inflation is worth only 95 cents at the end of a
year. A dollar in a no-interest checking account (or in a coffee
can under the bed) is worth even less.

Everybody should have some money in liquid assets (that
is, assets that are readily available for spending), but there are
safe, convenient money market accounts—many of which you
can write checks on—that pay higher interest rates than savings accounts. You can put your money in stocks or a mutual
fund and have a good chance of keeping up with inflation
and then some. And you would still be able to sell out quickly,
or borrow using your securities as collateral, if you ever need
cash for an emergency. Of course, your securities may be
worth more or less than you paid for them at that particular
point in time. It is incredible to me that Americans still keep
billions and billions of dollars in low-interest savings accounts.
Holding more than you need for day-to-day expenses in a sav-

ings or checking account is simply throwing away an opportunity, often in exchange for no extra safety or convenience.

Similarly, many people have accumulated substantial cash values in life insurance policies. The insurance companies are paying them negligible amounts of interest on that money. These policyholders can often borrow this money back from the insurance companies at relatively low rates and reinvest it elsewhere at a higher rate, locking in something pretty close to a riskless profit. Yet they don't do it, because (they say) they haven't gotten around to starting an investment program yet.

Other people invested in stocks at some period in the past and then put them aside, assuming they would continue to provide long-term growth or attractive income. But things change. Stocks that looked good ten years ago may be only mediocre investments today. Other stocks may have stronger growth possibilities, or they might be paying higher dividends.

It was great to own oil stocks in the mid to late 1970s, when there was a high inflation rate and the value of the companies' oil reserves was appreciating to keep up with it. But in the early 1980s, inflation slowed down and the price of oil had dropped. While some oil stocks remained good investments over this entire period, when I saw an investor in 1993 who owned a whole slew of oil stocks, I knew I was looking at an out-of date portfolio. Of course, in the year 2000, oil prices began shooting up again.

More recently, high tech has become the mantra for economic growth. High tech was going to save the country, and during much of the 1990s, any company that had something to do with the Internet watched its price get bid up in the stock market. Eventually, some of the excitement over Internet stocks had to die down, and indeed, in early 2000, the Internet sector underwent a correction, falling more than 50% from its highs. While the top-tier Internet stocks quickly began to bounce back, a lot of the secondary names may never recover. So eventually, Internet-heavy portfolios may look as outdated as those that focused on oil companies.

Investment portfolios have to be managed the way a wine lover manages her cellar or an orchard owner tends to his trees. Drink the mature bottles before they turn; prune the branches. You've got to examine your holdings on a regular basis and ask, "If I had the current market value of these investments in cash, would I buy the same investment back?" Sometimes the answer to that question is yes, but often it's not. If it's no, then you should act. If you wouldn't buy those investments back if you had their value in cash, then you shouldn't have them at all.

It doesn't matter what you paid for your holdings in the first place, by the way. If you bought a stock at $20 and it dropped to $10, you might be waiting for it to go back up. But why *should* it go back up? In reality, there is no reason in the world why it's any more likely to go from $10 to $20 than any other $10 stock. Your stock doesn't "remember" that it used to be at $20. There is no law of economics or any mystical force drawing it back up to $20 because it once occupied that lofty position. At $10 a share, it might be a good investment and worth holding, or it might not. But making that decision should have nothing to do with what it used to sell for.

Your Current Assets (Hidden and Otherwise)

Before you can go anywhere at all, you have to know where you are and where you want to go. This sounds as if it should be too elementary to mention, but many people flounder because, financially speaking, they never stop to figure out which way is up. Taking the time to determine where you are financially and where you want to go is the first step in financial planning and the first step toward achieving your goals.

What is your starting position? That is, how much do you own and how much do you owe? Odds are, your assets are greater than you think, making it possible for you to come up with money to invest.

When it comes to totaling up your assets, listing items like stocks and bonds and bank accounts is obvious. But what about your house? Many people tend to value a house at the amount of money they've put into it, or the amount they have paid off on their mortgage. The actual value of your house, however, is what you can sell it for, not what you paid for it. Its market value, minus the amount you owe on it, is your house's contribution to your net worth.

Other assets that are sometimes overlooked include accounts in payroll savings plans, the cash value of life insurance policies, security deposits on rented property, and vested interests in retirement plans. (The latter are especially valuable assets because they shelter current contributions from taxes and grow tax-free until retirement.)

Looking toward retirement, you should also consider the value of your expected Social Security benefits. There has been a lot of talk in recent years about the unsoundness of the Social Security system. It is indeed a fact that the money you pay into Social Security today is not set aside to pay you benefits when you retire. Instead, it is paid out to today's retirees. The system may be adjusted and modified, but it is not very likely that American society ten, twenty, or thirty years from now will simply let its elder members starve. (Aside from ethical or moral considerations, the political power of the growing numbers of older voters also lends substantial security to Social Security.) It is probably fair to assume that there will be some sort of retirement income payments from the U.S. government, and that is the equivalent of a substantial asset. These days, a typical retiree might collect $1,200 a month from Social Security. This is the exact equivalent of owning $180,000 worth of 8 percent government bonds.

A surprisingly large number of people can also expect to benefit someday from the natural transfer of assets that takes place as families age and elders pass away. Those who can anticipate receiving inheritances may protest that they don't want to count on that kind of thing, that they hope their parents and grandparents live a hundred years, enjoying the use of their own money all the while and leave behind just enough to cover cab fare to the funeral home. But people tend not to play things that close. A large percentage of older Americans own a home that is paid for and some life insurance. These assets, plus even a modest accumulation of savings, often amount to a substantial estate. A person who stands to benefit from such an estate is in a different financial position than someone who does not.

Similarly, parents of successful children have a reserve asset that may be drawn upon in hard times. In most societies of the past, children were looked upon as sources of security for one's old age. That's one reason why, even today, it is so difficult to persuade poor people in overcrowded countries to have fewer children. In America, the parents of successful children may protest that they would never take anything from their sons and daughters. Yet often those children say there is nothing that would give them more pleasure than helping their parents. Clearly, an elderly person with prosperous children is in a better financial position than one with no children. Parents of unsuccessful children, on the other hand, may have a continuing need to share their own assets with their offspring.

Other hidden assets include some items that at first glance look like expenses. Education, for one, may cost tens of thousands of dollars, but that is not an expense; it is an investment. Having an education is like owning a business; an educated person's increased skills and enhanced employability are going to make money for them. Similarly, spending money to raise and educate your children is an investment in human capital that may someday be valuable to you. And ultimately, money spent on improving a home or buying a vacation house may be viewed not as an expense but as an investment in real estate.

Even if you don't own a house, have not been to college, and have neither well-off parents nor well-off children, you still have yourself. You have a brain. You have intelligence. You have the ability to earn a living. Over your lifetime you will almost certainly earn more than $1 million. You are an asset.

Finally, you have an additional advantage because you had the good fortune to be born in, or the gumption to move to, a country where it is possible to accumulate wealth. In the United States, we take for granted certain prerequisites for economic success that are in short supply elsewhere. The stability of our government and economy give enduring value to the paper assets that are central to any investment program. In much of the world, people keep their savings in the form of gold or jewelry because they never know when the government might fall or the economy collapse. There may be limits on their freedom to invest their money as they like or to move it from market to market. And they may be concerned that the government might attempt to seize their property. These people do what they can to protect what they have, but gold bars hidden in a chimney are not earning any interest. That kind of wealth does not grow.

In stable societies like the United States, however, it is not foolhardy to trade one's wealth for a piece of paper, such as a bond, a stock certificate, or a savings passbook. You can have confidence that next year, and the year after that, those pieces of paper will still have value. This is an often unappreciated prerequisite for any investment program.

Our society also provides us with a highly developed infrastructure of roads, energy distribution systems, communications, and other essential support services for business and industry. If an entrepreneur has an idea for a new product, he can open a shop and start to produce it. He doesn't have to begin by digging a well and buying a generator. Nor does he have to teach newly hired employees how to count, or even how to program a computer. Our educational system turns out hundreds of thousands of qualified people each year in scores of fields. Human capital is available for any new enterprise.

That means if you have an idea, you can pursue it, and if it works, you can make a fortune on it. Horatio Alger is alive and well in this country. If you don't believe it, read about the rise of companies like Microsoft, Nike, Home Depot, or countless other successful new enterprises.

Maybe you don't have an idea that will make millions. Maybe you're not willing or able to turn a new idea into the next Microsoft. Not to worry. Making money in the United States is simplified by the fact that all around you people are making money. The American economy creates wealth at a vast and exponentially expanding pace.

The American economy is an immense productive machine. Even if it is growing more slowly than some of the emerging markets of Asia or Latin America, in absolute terms it is expanding at a rate that generates plenty of opportunities for companies, and those who invest in them.

The nation's record of steady growth over the decades has made Americans, even those with modest incomes, wealthy in historical and international terms. Poor people from Latin America, Asia, and elsewhere risk everything to emigrate into the United States, where any job will make them "rich" compared to those they left behind.

Americans of moderate means today enjoy luxuries that were beyond the reach of John D. Rockefeller, Sr. As rich as he was, Rockefeller could not travel from New York to Los Angeles in a few hours, in a vehicle that was cooled on an uncomfortably hot day, all the while dining on out-of-season tropical fruit and listening to the New York Philharmonic play whatever symphony he felt like hearing. A clerical worker with $400 for a discount airline ticket, a Sony Discman, and a pineapple from the nearest supermarket can enjoy what Rockefeller could only dream of.

In a country of such wealth, it is no remarkable thing to claim a piece of the action for oneself. Wealth is being created all around us. If we put our money to work in the investment market, we can help finance the process, and we can get our share of this new wealth.

Accumulating Something to Invest

But we must have some money to begin with. The first step toward investing is to amass some capital. As I explained before, the odds are that you already have some capital—in a savings account, life insurance policy, payroll savings plan, or elsewhere. That's why you need to take a good look at your assets. Developing a comprehensive financial plan will help you determine your investment possiblities. Of course, you might have no capital, or you very well might not have enough.

What you must do is divert some of your income from current consumption. Robert Louis Stevenson described one of the worthy goals of life like this: "To earn a little, to spend a little less." It is a hard prescription, but a necessary one. Ultimately, it can be very rewarding.

Giving up a little consumption now will provide you with the means for a great deal of consumption later, because of the way your investment will grow. As we saw in Chapter 1, just $2 a week diverted from buying lottery tickets can turn into $33,349. Playing the lottery may be fun, but is it $33,349 worth of fun? Most employed people *can* accumulate capital. But it does require the discipline of not spending everything you earn. (And it certainly requires the discipline of not using credit to spend money you have not yet earned.)

Many people plan on saving a certain portion of their income, say 10 percent. But that budget item is often the first thing to be cut when times are hard or when winter coats go on sale in January. (One way to forgo cutting it is to arrange for regular direct deposits from your paycheck or checking account into an investment plan.) You should resist all interruptions in your savings program. You should consider your commitment to save as being no less important than your commitment to make your mortgage payment or pay your telephone bill. After all, your future financial independence is just as important as your house or being able to call Uncle Willard in Albuquerque. That doesn't mean you should skip your mortgage payment to put the money into savings. But you should be just as reluctant to neglect saving as you would be to miss a mortgage payment. Obviously, in a true emergency, saving may have to be stopped or even dipped into, but, short of emergencies, you should treat your obligations to yourself with the same respect you accord your obligations to others.

Saving money is rarely an easy task. Living on less than you earn is difficult for working people. Asking people to begin an investment program by reducing their current standard of living may be perceived as unfair and doomed to failure. It is like putting someone on a crash diet. Such diets seldom work. The only way to take weight off—and keep it off—is to modify eating habits so that the dieter stays satisfied but eats less. If you can divert a portion of your income from consumption into investment without any problem, great. If you can explain the laudable purpose of your investment program to other members of your family and they cheerfully go along with it, swell. Otherwise, you might try this:

For the next twenty-four months, continue to live on your current income. You will probably receive a raise during the next year, but don't spend the extra money. Put it all into your savings program and continue to live on your pre-raise salary. This will not require any reduction in your standard of living. After all, you're *already* living on your current salary. (Actually, to the extent that prices go up, your standard of living will decline; fortunately, we have been in a low-inflation period in recent years.) When you get a second raise, then start living at the level of your first raise. And carry this on indefinitely. Always live at the level of the raise before last, and put all the proceeds from your latest raise directly into your investment program. To make this plan work, you have to get through just one raise period (generally one year) without improving your standard of living. Those twelve months of sacrifice, out of the six hundred or more months of your adult life, will make all the difference in the world to you. Do it, and you will be on your way to accumulating substantial wealth. Don't do it, and you will spend your entire life haunted by vague but insistent financial worries.

I believe it's fair to conclude that the first two years of a savings plan will demonstrate pretty conclusively whether or not you will someday achieve financial independence. If you start a savings plan, some unexpected expenses will arise. Unexpected expenses always arise. You will either use these inevitable unexpected expenses as an excuse to nibble away at your savings, or you will not. If you can get through two years without making excuses to dip into your savings, you will probably never make such excuses (and the money put aside during the first two years alone will grow into a substantial sum, thanks to compound interest). You will someday be financially independent. If you can't get through two years without making such excuses, then you probably can't get through the two years after that with your savings intact either. You might as well put down this book right now and resign yourself to a lifetime of just getting by.

The Importance of Starting Now

If you are going to begin an investment program, it is absolutely crucial that you do it soon, not just because of the dangers of procrastination but also because of the inescapable logic of mathematics. We have already had a look at the wonders of compound interest, but we should look again. With compound interest, a sum does not increase arithmetically; it increases geometrically. That means that money does not grow at the same rate forever. The longer it is held, the faster it grows. Eventually, it grows at a truly dizzying pace.

Consider, for example, the sum of $10,000 invested at age thirty-five and held until age sixty-five. At 10 percent compound interest, that $10,000 will grow to $174,494. If that same $10,000 were invested at age twenty-five, however, by age sixty-five it would have grown to $452,592. In other words, each dollar *not* invested at age twenty-five represents $45 you will not have at age sixty-five. The investments you make when you are young will be the most effective ones you ever make. This property of compound interest also points up the real tragedy of chasing after illusive get-rich-quick schemes. It's bad enough to lose the money you invest in those schemes; it's even worse to lose the years of relentless compounding that money could be enjoying if it had been invested prudently.

In some ways, it is relatively easy to save when you're young because you are unlikely to have expensive family obligations. On the other hand, when you're young there are so many things you would like to buy. The pain involved in *not* spending some of the money you earn can be eased—and this is true at any age—if you keep in mind that the money you save is not being taken from you forever. It is simply being diverted to buy something grander in the future. Do not think: "I am saving $4,000 this year that I could have used to buy an aboveground swimming pool." Think: "I am putting aside money for my future purchase of a vacation home in the mountains of North Carolina instead of buying an aboveground swimming pool."

You are not, after all, investing so that someday you can dive into a pile of money like Scrooge McDuck. (At least, you shouldn't be.) You are investing to do some very nice things for yourself and your family: buying that new home, sending your children to college, taking a world cruise, financing a midlife career change, making sure that you don't have to live in a single-room walk-up when you're seventy-five years old.

You should spell out exactly what your investment objectives are. This will not only make you feel better about putting money aside. It will also guide you toward the right kind of investments. Not every investment is appropriate for every purpose. You should make it clear to yourself and others exactly what it is you are investing for. How much money do you want? What do you want to accumulate money for? How much time do you have to reach your goals? Are you saving up money to pay for private school tuition in three years, or retirement in forty years?

When these questions have clear answers, when you're committed to creating a pool of capital by not spending everything you earn, and when you're prepared to treat your own savings program with the same respect you accord your obligations to the telephone company, then you are ready to begin.

For many people, it makes good sense to have a financial plan that can be updated as personal situations change. You can develop a plan on your own utilizing one or more of the financial software packages available today. But you are more likely to follow through with your plan and update it regularly if you develop it with your financial advisors. A financial plan will help you stick to your goals. It will serve as a reality check with regard to what you can expect from your financial decisions.

A good financial plan takes an objective look at your complete financial picture—from assets and liabilities to retirement savings, insurance coverage and estate plans. It takes into consideration your goals and objectives, including such factors as the age at which you want to retire, your investment risk tolerance, and whether you face large expenditures for your children's educations. A good plan is updated as financial and personal circumstances change so that you are always getting the most out of your assets.

CHAPTER 3

SETTING GOALS—AND

REACHING THEM

The Importance of Goals

Among the many investment books on the market, there was once one entitled *Die Rich.*

No thank you.

I have no objection to leaving a vast estate behind me when I go, but neither do I have any objection to leaving no estate at all. One owes one's children love, and support during the early years of their life, and enough education to prepare them to make their way in the world. One does not owe them continued support after dear old Mom and Dad pass on. If money is there for them when I'm gone, that's nice. But if I have to sacrifice enjoying my own life just to leave a bundle behind, no thank you. I'll leave them the family Bible, some photographs of myself, and my very best wishes for the future.

Now, you may feel differently. You may have a strong desire to create a family fortune. Or your financial goal might be to accumulate enough money to be the first person on your block to buy a helicopter. Or you may want to indulge in some "rich-man's graffiti" by leaving your alma mater a building with your name on it. Most likely, however, you want what most people want—the comfortable feeling of financial serenity.

You should have a goal, whatever it may be. Many people avoid setting goals for themselves for a very simple reason: People who have goals risk failure.

Whoever knows your goals (even if it's only you) will know if you fail to reach them. But people without goals can never fail. A goal is a challenge. It is easier not to have one.

It is also foolish not to have one. If you have a reasonable financial goal, or even a slightly unreasonable one, you can achieve it. Keeping a financial target fixed in your mind, especially if it's part of a financial plan, will help give you the discipline you will need along the way. If you have no goal, all of your income is likely to pass through your hands as you receive it, leaving you to trust in luck for the future. Moreover, having a goal will help clarify how you should manage your finances. Otherwise, as it says in *Alice in Wonderland,* if you don't know where you're going, there are many ways to get there.

It is worth stating your goal in very concrete terms. If your goal is to be rich, figure out what you mean by "rich." One

---

The Four Steps of Financial Planning

1. Examine where you stand financially today.
   - Review your assets and liabilities to determine your current net worth.
   - Determine your financial goals, timetables, and risk tolerance.
2. Identify where you are falling short in reaching your goals and develop a strategy to overcome these shortfalls.
3. Execute your plan consistently.
4. Revise your plan as personal and financial realities shift, to stay on target for reaching—and surpassing—goals.

person's life of luxury, after all, is another person's spartan existence. If you really think about it, you'll probably decide that you don't want to be *too* rich. If you suddenly inherited $100 million, odds are that you would lose most of your friends. Think about it. They would be envious of you; you wouldn't know if they loved you for yourself; they couldn't afford to go out to dinner with you at your new favorite Chinese restaurant—when it turns out be in Shanghai—and your new bodyguard would probably make them nervous. Besides, simply taking care of that much money is a full-time job. No time to go fishing if you have to keep a constant eye on the London, Zurich, and Singapore stock markets, as well as your investments in Malaysia and Argentina. So what's the point?

If you think about it carefully, you may conclude that your goal is to have a net worth of, say, $1 million by the time you turn sixty-two. If you're now in your thirties or thereabouts, this is an eminently realistic ambition. Specifying exactly what you're aiming at will enable you to calculate what you need to do to achieve it—how much you need to invest every year and what rate of return you need to earn on your investment. You will be able to chart your progress year by year and see when you are falling behind and when you are getting ahead.

Once you've calculated what you want and have seen what it will take to get it, you may even decide to change your goal. If reaching it requires that you invest $10,000 a year and the only way you can possibly put aside that much money is by continuing to work at a high-paying job you detest, then you probably ought to reconsider your goals. Is it worth being miserable for the next thirty years to be happy for the twenty years after that? What if you get hit by a bus the day after you retire? Maybe you should do something you like for the next thirty years, even though it means resigning yourself to a more modest way of life now and when you retire. Man does not live by bread alone, or by chocolate cake either.

Where Do You Stand?

The first step toward reaching your goal, whatever it is, is to establish your current net worth. You do that by adding up everything you own and subtracting everything you owe. Businesses figure out where they stand by drawing up "balance sheets." You should do the same. You can do it with a professional financial planner, but you can probably do a pretty good job of it on your own, too.

Begin by drawing a line down a piece of paper. On the left side list your assets—everything you own. List every asset at its current market value.

Your assets may include:

- Cash and cash equivalents
  - Checking/savings accounts
  - Money market accounts
  - Cash values of life insurance
- Investments
  - Stocks
  - Bonds
  - Mutual funds
  - Annuities
  - Limited partnerships
- Stock options
- Net value of your privately owned business
- Personal property such as
  - Your primary residence
  - Your vacation home
  - Automobiles
  - Other personal property (jewelry, furniture)
- Intangible or illiquid assets, such as:
  - Copyrights
  - Patents

Unfortunately, you can't stop there, although some people try to. How often have you read about fabulously wealthy people who suddenly go broke? They had the house in Beverly Hills and the chalet in St. Moritz, the Ferrari and the jewels, and the next thing you know they are standing in front of some judge saying it was drugs, or liquor, or illegal inside information that led them to ruin, and would their creditors consider settling up for $5,000 and the old Chevrolet the cook used to drive?

These people had a lot of assets, yes, but they had very little net worth. That's because of what was on the right side of the balance sheet.

The right side is where you list your liabilities, or everything you owe (including amounts you owe on the assets listed on the left side of the balance sheet). If you own a house worth $200,000 and you owe $80,000 on the mortgage, and you have $20,000 worth of stocks, and you owe your mother-in-law $5,000, your balance sheet would look like this:

Personal Balance Sheet

Assets		Liabilities	
Cash	$14,000	Mortgage	$80,000
House (market value)	200,000	Debt to Mom	5,000
Stocks	20,000	Car Loan	6,000
401(k) Plan Assets	30,000	Credit Card Bills	3,000
Personal Assets	4,000		
(jewelry, paintings, etc.)			
Total Assets	$268,000	Total Liabilities	$94,000

The total value of all your assets minus the total of all your liabilities is your net worth. In this case, that's $268,000 minus $94,000, or a net worth of $174,000. Not bad.

The Perils of "Pocket Accounting"

Most personal balance sheets are actually a good deal more complicated than this. But if you examine them carefully, balance sheets can show you not only how much you have but also how well it is distributed. It is generally advisable to have your assets diversified among several different types of investments. Many people don't, however, often as a result of what I call "pocket accounting." They've stashed some money away in one pocket for the kids' college education. They've set up a retirement fund in another pocket. And yet another pocket contains savings for next year's vacation. Meanwhile, they've just bought another life insurance policy besides the one they have already.

This is not the best way to organize your money.

Dividing up your funds in this multipocketed fashion may convince you that you're taking care of all your perceived financial needs. But in fact, divvying up your assets this way may distract you from the search for the most profitable ways to invest those funds. Or it may cause you to concentrate your investments too narrowly. Sure, only some of your retirement money is in the stock of one company, let's say GE, and only some of your children's education fund is in GE stock, and only part of your other investments are in GE stock. But if you look at it all together, you may find that GE had better keep selling a lot of lightbulbs because you've got more of your net worth concentrated in its stock than you realized.

Do you remember Christmas Savings Clubs? They used to be very popular. People were encouraged to prepare for their holiday gift buying by depositing a small amount in a special bank account every week. Just think, the bank advertisements crowed, you put in a mere $10 a week for fifty weeks, and at the end of the year you'll have $500! That is, in fact, exactly what many banks paid back to their Christmas Club depositor—just $500, *with no interest.* The depositors' focus on the specific objective of the savings program blinded them to its severe limitations.

Most people today are too sophisticated to dream of enrolling in a no-interest Christmas Club, yet, by neglecting to think about their assets as a unified whole, they may still be failing to maximize their investment returns. Some investments offer better returns than others without any additional risks, and those are the investments your money should be in. Although it may seem wise to divide up your money here and there for specific purposes, it's not. Money is money. Putting $5 a week in the cookie jar may indeed help you save up for a new refrigerator, but it shouldn't be asking too much of yourself to have the discipline to contribute your refrigerator money to an investment program where it will accumulate more than crumbs. You can still take money out to buy a refrigerator when the time comes; meanwhile, you've got money for other needs and you're able to manage it more efficiently and get better returns.

To see how pocket accounting may cause a family's funds to be improperly diversified, consider a couple whose primary assets are their stakes in company pension plans that will pay them $3,000 a month for life after they retire. In the meantime, they maintain bank accounts in their children's names which they set up years earlier to provide for their kids' college educations. Finally, both husband and wife have $100,000 term life insurance policies, to help the surviving spouse adjust to becoming head of a single-income family.

This couple's assets are not negligible, but they are badly distributed. Every one of their investments has an upper growth limit. Their $3,000-a-month pensions may seem adequate today, but by retirement time, inflation is likely to have substantially reduced its value. The children's bank accounts may be invested in certificates of deposit paying whatever is the current interest rate, but they will always earn that rate and nothing more. The $100,000 term insurance policies will never provide more than $100,000 in death benefits, and that, like the fixed pensions, may be decimated by inflation.

This couple should have a portion of their assets in stocks, and perhaps in real estate investments as well. Yes, these investments are riskier than the ones they have, but historically they have kept pace with inflation. Pocket accounting has caused this couple to put all their eggs in a limited-growth basket. Each investment seems right for its particular purpose. However, the big picture is that they've minimized the risk of losing money on their investments, but they haven't faced up to the risk of not having enough money.

Another common example of those with poorly diversified assets are people who are house-rich. Think of a couple who has raised a family in a four-bedroom house they have owned for nearly thirty years. Now the kids are gone, and the couple is alone. Over the years, their house has appreciated in value; it is now worth $300,000. All they owe on the mortgage is $25,000. Their only other assets are $25,000 in cash, stocks, and bonds. This couple may never have thought about it this way, but more than 90 percent of their assets are in a single real estate investment—their house. They may love the house dearly and want to stay in it no matter what. But on the other hand, once they realize the situation they are in, they might be perfectly happy to sell the house, buy a small condominium, and put the rest of the money into a well-diversified investment program that will generate cash for vacations and income for their retirement.

Thinking About Retirement

What about retirement? Since providing for a comfortable retirement is such an important and all-encompassing goal, doesn't it make sense to indulge in some pocket accounting for that?

The answer is yes, and no.

It certainly makes sense to take advantage of the excellent investment opportunities that have been created by the federal government to help people save for retirement. These plans are "tax advantaged." That is, they provide a way to avoid—or at least, delay—paying income tax on some current income. You should know about them, and you should take advantage of them.

Basically "tax-qualified" retirement plans involve a deal between you and Uncle Sam. The deal is that if you agree to put money away for your retirement in certain ways and not touch it, the tax collector will not impose any taxes on the money itself, or what is earned when this money is invested. When you retire and begin taking out some of that money, it will be taxed, but by then you may well be in a lower tax bracket. It's actually more complicated than that, but basically that's the deal, and it's an awfully good one. It would be foolish not to take advantage of it.

The 401 (k) Revolution

This social contract on retirement savings, this tacit agreement with Uncle Sam that says if you put the money away in prescribed ways, you can defer taxes on it—has become increasingly important to many Americans as a result of the defined contribution revolution. In the years after World War II, major American industries created their first pension plans and they were "defined benefit" plans. This meant that when you retired, the company would pay you a specific benefit: $1,100 a month, or half your last year's salary, or 60 percent of the average of your last five years' wages, or whatever. The company put aside money to pay that obligation when you retired, and the company took the risk that it would contribute too little over the years and would have to kick in more, or that it would contribute too much and have taken money out of the cash register that it could have used elsewhere.

As the 1980s began, however, "defined contribution" plans began to grow in popularity. Under these plans, an employee can elect to defer some of his or her income by making contributions to the plan, and the employer typically agrees to match some or all of this contribution. That money is invested, and when the employee retires, he or she gets benefits based on the amount that has accumulated in the investment fund. While the company's *contributions* are defined, the *benefits* no longer are.

The most prominent defined contribution plans are called 401(k) plans, after the section of the law that permits them. While 401(k) plans are offered to employees of businesses, those working for hospitals, schools, and other nonprofit institutions may be offered a similar alternative, called a 403(b) plan. The details of plans vary from one employer to another. Most notably, the amount and formula by which employers match contributions made by employees can differ significantly, depending on where you work. Although federal regulations limit employee contributions, the cap on contributions is indexed for inflation.

Whatever the amounts of money involved, many defined contribution plans shift the choice of investments and the investment risk from the employer to the employee. If the money put aside for you hasn't grown to a sum that will provide a nice retirement income, the company won't top off the fund, as they would in a defined benefit plan; that is now your responsibility. In return for foregoing a defined benefit, the employee often gets the right to choose how the money is invested and gets all the money that the investments earn, so astute investing can yield an attractive retirement income. In essence, the employee also gets immediate vesting in the retirement plan. Instead of waiting five years before being part of a company's retirement plan, as was the case with many defined benefit plans, every dollar you put aside in your defined contribution plan is yours at retirement, regardless of how long you stay with the company. However, there is usually a vesting schedule for any employer contributions.

As this century began, there were some 220,000 401(k) plans in the United States. They covered some 30 million workers and had total assets of more than $1.2 trillion. The defined contribution revolution has transformed the thinking of many employees. Instead of figuring their pension was something the company would take care of, millions of employees have had to take charge of their own futures. As a result, millions of Americans have had to become investors.

The typical defined contribution plan offers a set of investment alternatives. These often include several stock and bond funds, a money market fund, and some sort of contractual savings plan offering a predetermined return. If you're a participant in a defined contribution plan, it's your job to decide what mix of investments is right for you. The company will generally offer "education," but employers tiptoe around giving any outright advice for fear of being sued if the investments don't do well. So you're on your own.

One of the best things about 401(k) plans is that many employers match part or all of their employees' contributions, giving their employees an immediate guaranteed profit. If your employer offers such a plan, jump in. You can't go wrong taking someone else's money.

Another big advantage of 401(k)s is that the investment returns they produce are not taxed until they are withdrawn, which is often many years later. In the meantime, the money is left to compound tax-deferred. We've already seen how compound interest permits even modest investments to grow to enormous sums if enough time is allowed to elapse. Alas, for most investments, income tax must be paid on each year's investment income. This reduces the impact of compounding by reducing the amount of money that is left to compound. But that's not a problem in 401(k) plans or other "qualified" retirement plans.

Let's see what that means.

Suppose two sisters named Lisa and Jennifer each have $2,000 to invest. Both of them are in the 28 percent tax bracket. Both of them invest their money in securities earning a 10 percent return. But Lisa puts her money into a 401(k) while Jennifer invests on her own.

After one year, each will have earned $200 on her money. However, Jennifer's $200 is immediately taxed at 28 percent, and she only gets to keep $144. Lisa's $200, meanwhile, is inside her 401(k), so she not only puts aside money without having to pay income tax on it, she is not taxed on the return earned by that money. As the second year begins, Lisa has $2,200, while Jennifer has only $2,144. Another year goes by, and the siblings have earned another 10 percent on their money. Jennifer's earnings are taxed again; Lisa's are not. Lisa now has $2,420 while Jennifer has $2,298.

Many more years go by, and compound interest begins to work its magic. After twenty years, Jennifer's original investment has grown to $8,034. After thirty years, she has $16,102. After forty years, she has $32,272.

Not bad, but take a look at Lisa. After twenty years, she has $13,455. After thirty years, she has $34,898. And after forty years, she has $90,519. (This is from a single investment of $2,000, mind you.) After forty years, because her interest has not been taxed, Lisa's retirement savings are more than double those of her sister. It's true that Lisa must, ultimately, pay income taxes on her accumulated earnings as she withdraws them, but what she has gained from tax-deferred compounded growth over the years will far outweigh her belated tax burden. What's more, if Lisa takes withdrawals during her retirement years, she may keep an even greater amount since she will probably be in a lower tax bracket at that time than when she was working.

If Lisa puts $2,000 into her 401(k) *every* year, instead of just once, after forty years she will have $973,704. And that's not counting any matching contributions that her employer may have put into her account. If Jennifer also saves $2,000 and puts the $1,440 that is left after taxes into her non-tax-advantaged program, after forty years she will have $324,512. $973,704 vs. $324,512. You choose.

By the way, many 401(k) plans also offer opportunities to borrow money when you need it. You can borrow to buy a house, pay for medical emergencies, or finance your children's education. Some plans don't ask what the money is for; they just lend it to you. It's cheaper than taking a loan from a bank, but remember it's your money you're borrowing, and what you use today is money that won't be there when you retire. You're also incurring a cost because all of the money you've borrowed is no longer earning interest or dividends (and on a tax favored basis); instead of being invested, it's paying for that motorboat you're riding around in.

Remember the IRA

For many people, the key component of their retirement income will be their employer's pension plan, but don't forget the individual retirement account (IRA). Congress created IRAs in 1974 for individuals who had no employer pension plan. In 1981, the law was changed so that everybody, even those covered by pension plans, could have IRAs. Millions of Americans of all income levels realized that the IRA was a great deal, and by 1986, 40 million people had put $250 billion into IRAs. Tax legislation in the mid-1980s put a number of limitations on IRAs. But legislation in 1997 both enhanced the availability of Traditional IRAs and created two new kinds of IRAs: the Roth IRA and the Education IRA. (The latter is a bit of a misnomer; it's not really a retirement savings vehicle but rather a way of putting aside money for a child's education.)

While there is now an array of IRAs, they all share one important attribute: Money in an IRA grows on a tax-deferred basis; that means you don't pay any taxes on dividends, interest, or capital gains earned within the IRA. Of course, Uncle Sam gets his share in the form of taxes on money that's either going into an IRA or coming out. Contributions to a traditional IRA may be tax deductible, but when you withdraw money it's taxable as ordinary income. By contrast, contributions to a Roth IRA aren't tax deductible, but if you keep the money in the account for more than five years after your first Roth IRA contribution and meet other requirements, distributions will not be taxed.

Whichever kind of IRA you choose, they are a good way for you and your spouse to each put away up to $2,000 per year on a tax-deferred basis—a benefit that can be worth tens of thousands of dollars over the long run.

Let's go back to our example of Lisa and Jennifer. If their brother, let's call him Ira, chooses to put money into an IRA, he will come out somewhere between the two sisters. Assuming his IRA contributions are not tax-deductible at his income level, then like Jennifer, if he wants to invest $2,000, he must accumulate $2560 and pay federal income taxes of $560 on it. But, unlike Jennifer, Ira's investment compounds on a tax-deferred basis, so his account will show a balance of $701,067 after forty years. He's $273,000 behind Lisa, but he's $376,555 ahead of Jennifer, all because he invested in an IRA. Those who say an IRA isn't worth doing are blowing smoke. Anything that lets you accumulate money on a tax-deferred basis is almost always worth doing.*

IRAs do have some restrictions that you should be aware of before you start one. Generally, you may not withdraw any money from the account before you reach the age of 59½ without paying a ten percent penalty on top of any income tax due on the money withdrawn. However, these penalties may not be applicable in the case of contributions that weren't tax-deductible in the first place. Nor are there penalties on money withdrawn to pay certain medical expenses, qualified higher education expenses, first time home purchases (up to a $10,000 lifetime limit) or because you have become disabled.

Other Retirement Plans

For some taxpayers, there are still other tax-advantaged opportunities available. The federal government allows self-employed individuals to establish "Keogh" plans, which work like IRAs but permit those who qualify to make deposits of up

---

*All of these examples assume that the siblings always earn ten percent per year on their investments and that tax rates will never change. Obviously, if these assumptions change, the results will differ. But as long as the three siblings each get the same annual investment returns, it is important to note that Lisa will always do better than Ira and both will do much better than Jennifer because their investment returns are compounding free of taxes.

to 25 percent of their earned incomes (to a maximum set at $30,000 in 2000, for example) every year. Self-employed people can actually benefit doubly. They can have both Keogh plans and IRAs. In 1997 a new alternative called "SIMPLE" retirement plans were created for small business owners. There are also several other kinds of retirement plans for the self-employed that are like Keoghs in many ways. If you're self-employed that you need to talk to your accountant or tax advisor about which ones suit your situation.

And there are annuities. Annuities, which are offered by securities firms, insurance companies, and commercial banks, have become very popular because they provide the same benefits as employer pension plans—you can put away money to compound on a tax-deferred basis, and not pay taxes until you draw money out of the plan later on. In contrast to 401(k)s, Keogh plans, or old-style, pre-1986 IRAs, the money going into an annuity is not tax-deductible. But it compounds on a tax-deferred basis, so it inevitably accumulates to more than would a non-tax-deferred investment. (There is more on annuities in Chapter 5.)

I know it's hard to think about retirement when you're twenty-five years old. But that's the best time, because the longer your money accumulates, the more it can grow. Force yourself to look at the statistical realities: People are living longer and longer, and they're healthy longer and longer. A half century ago, retirement meant you quit working at sixty-five, sat on your porch and rocked for a couple of years, and then died; so how much money did you need? Now retirement may be at age fifty-five or sixty-two or sixty-five, or whenever you choose. You're likely to be retired for twenty years for sure, maybe thirty. Maybe you'll be retired longer than you worked.

And retirement doesn't mean sitting and rocking, it means trips and cruises, tennis and golf, moving to Florida or Arizona, volunteer work and hobbies. All of that takes money. Social Security and a pension from your job may take care of the basics, but the only way to make sure you have the money needed for a comfortable retirement is to take charge of saving it yourself. The federal government has provided a variety of mechanisms for saving that money on a highly tax-efficient basis. But it's up to you to take advantage of these opportunities. It's never too early to start saving for retirement; it can be too late, though.

While saving for retirement is critical, you should not succumb to pocket accounting and think of your retirement planning completely in isolation from the rest of your investments. While money in formal retirement plans should not be, and often cannot be, touched, you should still consider it part of your investment portfolio. That means that when you select investments for your 401(k) or Keogh or IRA, you should make certain that they balance your non-retirement investments for proper diversification. Your "retirement funds" are not entities in themselves; they are cohesive parts of the overall plan by which you are going to achieve financial serenity.

Eight Steps to Investment Success

Before I get into the specifics of selecting and managing investments, let's quickly review the outline of what you will need to do:

1. Convert income dollars to capital dollars. This is just another way of saying that you must spend less than you earn. Capital (as in capitalism) is required to begin any kind of investment program. Once you have amassed some capital by saving, then your money can begin to make money for you. No capital, no investment income.

2. If it's not already too late, start while you're young. As we have seen, the phenomenon of compound interest delivers its most fantastic rewards to those who put their money to work for the longest time. At a 10 percent rate of return, a single dollar invested at age thirty-five will grow to $17 by age sixty-five. That same dollar, invested at age twenty-five, would grow to $45 by age sixty-five. Whatever age you are now, your investment fund will grow larger if you begin it today instead of a week from Tuesday. You should start as soon as you finish this book. Better yet, as soon as you finish this chapter.

3. *Have a financial plan and update it regularly.* Calculate where you are and where you want to go. Understand how much your money must grow each year to enable you to reach your goal. Monitor your progress and revise your plan as conditions change.

4. *Be realistic.* Make sure you understand and accept, both intellectually and emotionally, that it will not be possible for you to find $10 stocks that go to $15 in six months. Ten-dollar stocks that go up $1 in a year while paying an annual dividend of 50 cents are what you can realistically expect to find most of the time. But they will do quite nicely for you. Given enough time, they will make you a small fortune.

5. *Be patient and disciplined.* It will take many years of compounding for your investments to grow. Don't be tempted to take risky shortcuts because you are bored. Do not let greed cause you to divert your money into get-rich-quick "sure things." If a cyclical market downturn sends your investments in the wrong direction, don't panic and sell out. But if your investments have been successful for a number of years, don't arrogantly decide that you've figured out the financial world and attempt to do something "clever." Stick to your plan.

6. *Avoid flat years.* Your plan envisions that your investments will grow by a certain percentage every year. If your goal is 10 percent annual growth, and one year you chase some wild goose and don't make a cent, then the following year your money must grow by 20 percent to get back on course. (Actually, it would have to grow by 21 percent, because the 10 percent growth you missed the previous year would itself have contributed one percent growth via com-

pounding.) Reaching your normal investment goal every year is likely to be difficult enough; doubling it because you missed a year is likely to be impossible.

7. *Avoid major life disruptions.* This is easier said than done, but that makes it no less important. Your financial plan is apt to be fatally derailed if at the age of fifty you decide to chuck your career and run away to Tahiti. You may make major lifestyle changes, but try to stay committed to your plan. One way or another, you're still going to have to educate your children and pay for your retirement. Stay the course.

8. *Leave it to the power of compound interest to generate your wealth.* Remember that you are investing for the long term. Remember that you are *investing*, not speculating.

What you are attempting to do is invest your money in enterprises that are creating wealth. If you can do that, you don't need to chase after short-term speculative profits.

And you *can* do that. In America, it is not difficult to find wealth-creating enterprises. The nation's dynamic economic system keeps changing, and new industrial titans keep emerging. Companies like Microsoft make fortunes not only for their creators but also for those who invest in them. The economy keeps changing, but those changes mean opportunities, not only for new companies that are created to capitalize on changes, but also old ones that are nimble enough to evolve.

Over the course of the modern history of the American economy, through booms and recessions, the average rate of growth of American corporations has been about 10 percent. This has been triple the average rate of inflation. Real profits have been made. Real wealth has been created. This process has brought immense benefits not only to the managers and employees of these companies but to their investors as well.

The rest of the world has taken notice of this success. Today most of the world's former Communist countries are eagerly attempting to imitate the market-oriented economic policies of the United States. Most of the developing nations of Asia, Latin America, and Africa are now equally enthusiastic about market-oriented policies like those that have served the U.S. so well. Today, there are far more stock markets than there were a quarter century ago and far fewer Communist parties. There's a lesson in that.

CHAPTER 4

SEEKING HELP

The Fallible Experts

Years ago, the New York *Daily News* asked one of my colleagues to participate in something called the "Battle of the Brokers." Each contestant was given a hypothetical $30,000 to invest any way he wished. Whoever had made the most money after two months was the winner.

My colleague won. He had an idea that interest rates were about to decline, and he invested his stake in securities that would go up if they did. They did—and the value of his securities increased 26 percent in just two months.

Three other investment professionals who took part in the competition did not fare so well. All three are well respected and have had years of experience on Wall Street. All three actually lost money during the test.

Only one other entry showed a profit. That was the *Daily News* Dart Fund, so named because it was a portfolio of stocks selected by *Daily News* reporters throwing darts at a stock table pinned to the office wall. Ten darts were thrown, and the ten stocks they landed on were purchased. The Dart Fund finished the contest in a respectable second place. It appreciated

3.4 percent in two months, which is equivalent to annual growth of more than 20 percent. This was one of a number of contests pitting professional stock pickers against the darts thrown at the stock market page of a newspaper.

Does this mean that you should throw away this book and buy a package of darts? Probably not. A dart can't tell you about the specific features of an investment, or the risks, or the tax consequences. Or whether you would be comfortable with them.

What the success of the Dart Fund should tell you is that nobody knows for certain what the market is going to do, especially over the short term (and two months is definitely short term). If you're looking for quick profits, you probably would do just as well to throw a dart as consult an expert.

But wait a minute, you say, aren't there a number of renowned authorities who have made fortunes for investors (and themselves) by telling people what to buy and what to sell, week by week and month by month?

Let me answer that question by introducing you not to a package of darts, but to a bag of coins. Imagine that every morning you take the coins out of a bag and ask them to tell you where the stock market is going that day. To find out what the coins think, you flip them. If they come up heads, that means the market will go up, while tails means it will fall.

About half the coins will come up heads and half tails. You note which ones came up heads and which came up tails. At the end of the day, you check to see how the market did and then you get rid of all the coins that made the wrong prediction: If the market went down, you put all those that came up heads in the piggy bank.

The next morning you take out the remaining coins and ask for another prediction. At the end of the day, again, about half will be winners and half will have incorrectly forecast the market. After the next day, about half the remaining coins will be gone, and the next day, half again, and so on. After a few days, there will be one coin that will have correctly predicted which way the market would go that day. You would have made a fortune if you had bought or sold on that coin's "advice."

What do you think the odds are that this wonderful coin will be right again on the next day? Would you bet money on it? You know that despite your coin's good forecasting record, it doesn't really know where the market is going when it comes up heads or tails. You'd like to think you've got a "lucky" coin. But you know you're just seeing the laws of probability theory being played out.

Someday you may encounter an investment advisor who has been right a dozen times in a row. He or she may be a person of unusual brilliance who is going to be right forevermore. Or he or she may only have been lucky. There are, after all, thousands and thousands of investment advisors and market forecasters at large in the land. The laws of probability apply to them just as they do to coins.

This doesn't mean that you should go it alone in the financial world, especially if you think you don't know much about it. With all due modesty, I have to tell you I know a *lot* about investments—I've been in the investment business for more than fifty years, and I'd like to think I've learned a thing or two—and *I* employ the services of a broker to help me make investment decisions. I turn to my financial advisor because his time is devoted, day after day, to following the securities markets, while I am often busy with other matters.

You will inevitably need a brokerage account to execute your investment decisions, even if you make those decisions on your own and you want to trade on-line. Whether you're buying or selling a stock or a bond, a rental property or a house, you cannot transact this kind of business by standing on a street corner with a sandwich board saying things like IBM SHARES FOR SALE.

More important, the right kind of advice can give you an edge over flipping coins or throwing darts. Half of those coin flips will always be wrong. The advice you can get from an investment professional will not always be correct, but if it's correct just 55 percent of the time, over the years you will be

significantly better off with it than without it. A professional
advisor may not always point you in the direction of the best
investment, but he or she is likely to help you avoid many of
the worst investments. The key to achieving these modest but
important advantages over even odds is to avoid asking questions that cannot be answered—such as "What is the market
going to do tomorrow?"—and to understand the limitations
of all predictions.

The Unpredictable Market

Suppose that you try to do it all by yourself. You take to
studying the financial pages of your local newspaper, and
you subscribe to the *Wall Street Journal, Fortune,* and *Forbes.* You
faithfully watch "Wall Street Week," CNBC, and "The Nightly
Business Report." You read books about the Federal Reserve
System and syndicated columns about the money supply.
Your spouse wants to know why you mention Alan Green-
span's name in your sleep.

Where does it all get you?

You will become an educated person with an excellent
understanding of the forces at work in the economic world
around you. You will gain insights into the relationships
between interest rates, inflation, and the prices of various
investments. You will be able to avoid making some stupid
mistakes, and spitting into the wind. You may even become a
happier and a more confident person.

But there are limits to how much you can learn. The investment markets have grown increasingly complicated in recent
years. A variety of new investments have been created, and
each of them has their pros and cons. Although the United
States has the largest financial market in the world, more and
more investors have recognized that there are attractive investment opportunities in other countries as well. If you're interested in stocks, there are not only all those listed stocks but a
steady stream of new ones coming to market, and thousands

that are not traded on major exchanges, and thousands more that have been doing well in countries that you probably didn't know had a stock market.

So you decide to read even more. But you still will not *know* what's going to happen tomorrow to the price of anything because many prices are unpredictable. Who knows when a factory will burn down, a visionary CEO will quit, or a product will suddenly be found to have a major defect? Yet any of those events could have a major impact on a stock. Who knows when fickle teenagers will quit spending millions on expensive sneakers and decide they want to take up the outdoors look. Many of these things are unknowable. Maybe you know a palm reader who can foresee the future. Some people have a better perspective on economic matters than others, but remember nobody really *knows* the future.

And no matter how much you read, other people know how to read too. By the time you pick up the morning *Wall Street Journal* and read that United Sprockets has just been awarded a $10 billion government contract, a couple of million other people already know about it. Some of them got their paper before you did. Some of them saw the news on the financial wire the day before. Most significant, a lot of them *expected* this to happen. They knew that the Defense Department was running short of sprockets. They knew that United Sprockets was a contender for the contract.

That's why stocks often fall when good news is announced. The good news has been anticipated and was *already* built into the price of the stock. In most cases, this does not mean that "insiders," such as corporate officials and their friends, have been trading illegally on the basis of inside information. This does happen, and there are a number of celebrated insider-trading cases. However, usually the prospects of individual companies are foreseen, completely legally, by people whose job it is to keep track of developments in various industries. Such people don't have to wait to read a newspaper article to find out what's going on. They can talk to the same people the reporter talks to.

Economists have a theory to explain why you cannot predict which way stock prices will move. (It would be nicer if they had a theory that *could* predict which way prices will move; a theory explaining why that's impossible seems like a poor consolation prize to me.) They call it the "efficient market hypothesis." It says that in an efficient market—and the U.S. stock market is one—the significance of new information is quickly transmitted to market participants and is immediately reflected in prices.

Thus, at any point in time, the prices in the market reflect all that is known—and knowable—about that stock. The speed with which information affects prices may seem miraculous. (The classic economics textbook by Paul Samuelson and William Nordhaus cites a study that found that you could profit from stock-related news only if you bought or sold the stock within thirty seconds after the news was first made public.)

There's nothing magical about this. It results from the fact that thousands of very smart and diligent people are constantly looking out for information that will affect stock prices, and some of them inevitably are finding it and acting on it. Of course, stock prices will still be driven up and down by totally unexpected news, like a gas leak that sends United Sprockets' main factory up in flames. But it's awfully hard to profit from that kind of news. If it's unanticipated, by definition, you cannot anticipate it. And if it can reasonably be anticipated, rest assured that thousands of professional securities analysts and portfolio managers will have anticipated it. It's certainly too late to act by the time you see the story in the next day's newspaper or even hear a news flash on the radio.

Despite all this, there is no shortage of people prepared to tell you exactly what the market is going to do in the near future—for a price. Expensive newsletters published by stock market seers can be yours if you want them. There are so many of these newsletters that there's even a newsletter that does nothing but keep track of the success or failure of the recommendations published in dozens of other newsletters. Some of these seers have been right several times in a row. (Some of them have been right, by the way, because their prophecies are self-fulfilling: They have so many followers that when they recommend a stock, their own followers' purchases drive the price up, at least temporarily.) But always remember that past success does not mean that tomorrow morning's prediction will be accurate. Maybe the next flip of the coin won't forecast the market after all.

Ultimately, the most useful investment advice has nothing to do with what is going to happen to the market tomorrow. Instead, it focuses on the fundamental underlying value of securities you are considering purchasing, and the degree to which any prospective investment suits your own particular situation and goals. There are people qualified to give you this kind of advice. You would be wise to employ their expertise.

Selecting a Financial Advisor

Investment advice is available at many places these days. It used to be a lot simpler. Once, you could buy insurance only from an insurance agent, real estate only from a real estate agent, and stocks and bonds only from a securities broker, and you had to have a bank account in order to write checks. But the lines between various financial institutions have broken down as a result of deregulation. Today, for example, banks sell stocks and life insurance, life insurance companies sell mutual funds, and most Wall Street brokerage firms sell a wide array of investments as well as insurance and various forms of credit, including home mortgages. Moreover, many investment accounts offer check-writing features, just like a bank account.

This is all to your benefit, since a "stockbroker" or "insurance agent" or "banker" who now has many financial products to sell will be able to select freely from among them to find the ones that suit you best.

Instead of looking for advice, of course, you could spend all of your waking hours studying investments. You could, that is, if you didn't have to earn a living and didn't mind competing with firms that have thousands of full-time employees collectively studying what you were trying to cover single-handedly.

Most people quite properly view their investments as a bit of a sideline; their principal economic focus is their career. But at the same time, they know that their investments are important. And they know they should get some professional advice about their investments, just as they do with regard to legal and tax matters. You use a lawyer and an accountant when you need one; you see dentists and doctors rather than treating your own ailments. So why go it alone on investments?

You have many choices, but none of them are simple. You could hire an investment manager to take care of your money. But there are some twenty-two thousand registered investment advisors in this country, and you would have to study their track records and their investment styles to see what suits you. And, many have high minimum-account requirements, anything from $25,000 at a bare minimum up to $5 million. You could invest in mutual funds, in which professional managers pool your money with money from other investors and invest in a diversified portfolio of securities. But there are now more mutual funds than there are stocks listed on the New York Stock Exchange, and choosing funds on your own has become a complicated and time-consuming task. You could hire a financial planner—there are thousands of them, with widely varied expertise and independence.

For many people, working with a stockbroker is an effective way of building and managing a portfolio of investments. Brokers, financial advisors, registered representatives—whatever a securities firm calls them these days—advise you on selecting and managing a portfolio of investments. They can also help you select mutual funds or identify a money manager.

While some people want to go it alone, I'm a firm believer in having a trusted broker to serve as investment advisor as well as to execute investment orders. Of course, you protest, since I once headed one of the largest full-service investment firms, what would you expect me to say. But I would turn that around and say the reason I was proud to have led such a firm is because I believe this is the way the average investor can get the best results. That's why I think it is as critical for you to find and work with a good broker as it is for you to find and work with a lawyer, accountant, or pediatrician whom you like and trust.

Brokers are, of course, generally paid on a commission basis, and it is in their interest to sell you something. But a broker who has many different investment vehicles to offer will earn a commission no matter what you buy; there will usually be less incentive to steer you toward something unsuitable. And a broker who is astute should realize that he or she is better off in the long run having satisfied customers who come back for more, rather than aggrieved clients who badmouth them all over town. The best source of new accounts is referrals from happy customers. Moreover, in recent years, a growing number of securities firms have implemented programs that compensate brokers based on the value of your assets, not on a per-transaction basis.

There is no fixed prescription for finding a broker who is right for you. It is largely a matter of chemistry. An important part of your relationship with a broker depends on how you feel about him or her, so choosing a broker involves aspects of personality that cannot be quantified. (How did you choose your doctor? Your veterinarian? Your auto mechanic?) You might begin by asking friends for recommendations. Or you can simply march into the office of a reputable brokerage firm and ask them what they can do for you.

There is, by the way, no reason to feel shy about walking unannounced into a broker's office because you're afraid you don't have enough money to invest or don't know enough to ask the right questions. Many brokers will be glad to see you, even if your means are modest, because a small client today might become a major client tomorrow. And even if you're not in a position to buy any stocks or bonds right now, they might be able to help you (and themselves) by putting your cash into a money market account or starting you off with small monthly investments in a mutual fund.

You've surely noticed all those television ads that feature homespun scenarios touting the benefits of one brokerage firm over another. Brokerage firms don't spend millions of dollars paying for commercials because they don't want people to drop by.

When you first enter a brokerage office, you might ask to speak to the manager. This person sets the tone for the place, so his or her attitude and answers to your questions will give you a quick sense of whether you have knocked on the right door. If the manager is not available, you may be introduced to whoever is taking "walk-ins" that day. Whomever you meet, feel free to talk for a while. And feel equally free to say good-bye.

You should talk to prospective brokers as if you were interviewing them for a job. You are—for the job of being your personal investment advisor. This is, needless to say, an important position, so you should take care in deciding whom you hire.

Beware, first of all, of any broker who promises you too much. He or she should talk at least as much about the risks of investing as about its rewards. He or she should not imply that the process of accumulating capital will be quick or easy. He or she should not have definite answers to your questions (but should have strong opinions). If a broker implies that he or she can spot $10 stocks that will go to $15 in six months, or that he or she can substantially increase the value of your holdings by frequent trading in and out of various securities, run, don't walk, to the next candidate.

You want a broker who wants to know a lot about you— how much you earn, how much you save, what your tax status is, what your investment goals are, how much time you have to achieve them, how much risk you can afford to take, and how much risk you feel comfortable taking.

You also want a broker who will make a commitment to devising a well-diversified investment program to help you meet your goals and who will monitor your investments after you've purchased them. He or she needs to review them periodically for continued suitability, instead of just selling you something and disappearing from your life forever.

You want a broker who will provide leadership for you as you move toward your goals, who will guide your actions, who will restrain you when your investments are plummeting and you want to sell out in a panic, and restrain you again when your investments are soaring and you decide you've figured out the secrets of Wall Street. You should not be embarrassed to accept the guidance of another person in an area as personal as your own finances. It is simply good management to rely on the specialized knowledge of others in fields where you are an amateur. Successful business executives do it all the time. You must be comfortable, however, with your broker's style of leadership. This is a matter of taste. One person's inspiring guide is another person's strutting Bonaparte. Choose as you will.

You want a broker, finally, who will help you develop realistic expectations for the progress of your investment program and who will help you establish yardsticks to measure whether those expectations are being met. You will not find, nor should you expect to find, a financial miracle worker. Those few brokers who are true geniuses are quickly promoted to senior executive positions at their firms, or develop very lucrative careers handling the accounts of very rich people and are soon spending much of their time improving their golf game in the Hamptons. They will not be saying hello to drop-in customers at a neighborhood brokerage office.

But this is no reason to despair. All you want—all you need—is a broker who will do a good, honest, average job of handling your affairs. Remember, the *average* annual appreciation of stocks in all American corporations during most of the twentieth century was slightly more than 10 percent. A broker who can get you that return year after year will be doing a very nice job of leading you toward your financial goals. But not every broker will be able to get that return for you. Half of all investments, after all, turn out by definition to be below average.

The difficulty of achieving even average returns has been dramatically demonstrated in recent years by the performance of the professional money managers who handle the accounts of huge pension funds and other multimillion-dollar clients. Year after year, studies have found that a majority of these professional money managers fail to equal the performance of the Standard & Poor's 500 Stock Index (a measure that is more representative of market movement than the better-known Dow Jones Industrial Average, which tracks only thirty stocks). As a result, some investors have given up trying to outperform the averages; they simply invest their money in portfolios consisting of every stock used to compile the averages. In this way, they guarantee that their performance will always be exactly "average," never above the market, but, more important, never embarrassingly below. This technique is known as the "index fund" approach.

So don't look down your nose at average performance. If you find a broker who can help you do just a little bit better than average, then you will be sitting pretty indeed.

One way a broker can help you is by calling on the resources of the brokerage firm's research department. That department will be made up of securities analysts who devote all their time to investigating the outlook for various investment possibilities. They can help you come up with ideas for new investments and decide when it might be time to sell existing ones.

They are awash in data. Sometimes, in fact, they appear to be operating on the belief that if data is tortured sufficiently, it will confess. Their discoveries are as fascinating as they are endless. Securities analysts have found, for example, that for many years there was a startling correlation between the movement of the stock market and the winner of the Super Bowl. Whenever the Super Bowl was won by a team with its roots in the original National Football League, the stock market went up during the following year. Every time the game was won by a team from the old American Football League, the market went down. That was a wonderful market indicator—until it stopped being true. Similarly, correlations have also been discovered between the level of women's hemlines and the stock market (rising hemlines signal rising stock prices) and between major league baseball batting averages and the stock market. (If the overall average in the majors goes down from the previous year, the market often goes up, and vice versa. Analysts have suggested that batters may not be inclined to wear themselves out squeezing out a hit when they are making big money in the stock market without getting winded.)

All of this is great fun, but it's not the kind of investment research data you can or should rely on. Nor is it what the research departments at securities firms focus their attention on. What they do is prepare careful analyses of publicly held corporations. Your broker will make these reports available to you. These analyses often provide solid indications of the long-term potential of the stocks in question. No matter how solid the research, you should not be overly confident that high-rated stocks will inevitably go up in price. After all, somebody else's research department may have reached the same conclusion last week and already driven up the price of the stock.

Ultimately, what is probably the most valuable service a research department can provide you is help in avoiding losers. While the researchers are uncovering well-managed companies with bright futures, they will also be coming across poorly managed turkeys. If your investments are well diversified, the growth of your portfolio will tend to approximate

the average. If you can avoid just one or two losers, your portfolio will grow a little bit better than average, and this will be
very nice.

Your portfolio would also grow a little bit better if you
didn't have to pay your broker, but commissions and fees are
a fact of life. Compared to commissions on real estate and
other valuable assets, securities brokerage commissions are
quite low. Nevertheless, those who want them lower still have
been attracted in recent years to "discount brokers," who
charge 30 to 70 percent less than traditional full-service brokers. Discount brokers are cheaper than full-service brokers
because they do not provide the range of services of traditional full-service brokers. You gather information and make
investment decisions on your own and then call them up and
tell them what you want to buy or sell. They buy or sell it for
you and send you a confirmation. End of transaction. End of
relationship. You don't even have to talk to a real person; by
the mid-1990s, a number of discount brokers communicated
with their customers via the Internet. In the late 1990s, several traditional brokerage firms also began offering on-line
services as well, including the ability to trade on-line at dis-
counted rates or for a set fee based on assets.

Not surprisingly, it is sophisticated investors who can
benefit the most from discount and on-line brokers. These
are people who have the confidence, time, experience, and
perhaps the hubris to make all of their own investment decisions. They know what they want to buy and sell and when.
"Our customer profile," the founder of the nation's largest
discount broker told the *New York Times,* "shows that 57 percent have been in the market for ten years, and 60 percent
spend five hours a week on their portfolios."

Most investors, including all beginners, will be a lot more
comfortable dealing with a full-service broker, who will provide them with research materials, explanations, and advice as
well as follow-up monitoring of their investments, and, yes, a
little psychological hand-holding.

The Broker–Client Relationship

A well-established and very successful broker I know tells this story of how he was approached by his best friend when he was first starting out in the business:

"My friend had a relatively small amount of money to invest, about $6,000, which was just about what I had in my own portfolio. He asked me if I wanted to play with his account. I said I did not want to 'play' with it. I was very serious about investing. I knew that if we played with it, we would lose it. And I didn't want to be the one he associated with losing his money.

"I suggested instead that we do some things with the money that would be extremely dull. And he got mad and said, 'I'll go someplace else.' And he did.

"About a year later, he called me and asked if I would help out his mother, who was recently widowed. She had a small nest egg that she couldn't afford to 'play' with. He asked me how my own account was doing. I told him, 'Fine—I've still got the same positions I had a year ago. How's your account doing?' He told me the broker he'd gone to had a lot of bright ideas and had him in and out of quite a few stocks over the year. When all was said and done, my friend had a lot of adventures, and he'd paid a lot of commissions—and his portfolio was worth about $4,500. He brought the money to me, and started a very dull process of slow, long-term growth."

This broker had been wise enough not to take on his friend as a client at a time when their relationship clearly would have been a failure. Only when they saw eye-to-eye on an investment philosophy could they begin to work together.

Your relationship with your broker is likely to play a significant role in your life. A successful broker–client relationship may last for many years and be profitable for all involved. An unsuccessful one will make everyone miserable. To try to make yours work, you should be sure that you and your broker share the same goals, and you should understand what you can expect from your broker, and what you cannot.

One thing that you should get from your broker is investment education. Your broker should be willing to explain to you exactly why he or she is recommending a particular investment, what he or she expects to happen to that investment, and when. If your broker expects the investment to achieve its growth over a long time frame (as he or she generally should), explaining this to you should help relieve you of worries about the "noise" of short-term up-and-down market movements. If the investment fails to perform as expected when its time has come, your broker should discuss with you why this occurred and work with you in formulating a new plan of action.

All of this should not only be educational. It should also be enjoyable. Many people thoroughly relish participating in the investment process—discussing their investments with their broker, charting their progress, and analyzing their results.

You must always keep in mind, however, that you are not your broker's only client. Your broker may indeed enjoy chatting with you. He or she should certainly be dedicated to giving you the best possible advice in a timely fashion. But he or she is likely to be equally dedicated to earning a decent living. If your broker breaks off conversations with you when you shift the topic from investments to the Red Sox, don't be insulted. (In fact, if your broker has plenty of time to discuss the Red Sox with you, then you should begin to worry. Why doesn't he or she have anything better to do?)

What kind of client does a broker like best? My broker friend describes his own all-time favorite: "He would call me and say, 'Good morning. What can you do for me today that will improve my account?' That really opened the door for me. Often, I could answer his question by saying, 'The best thing to do today is nothing.' And he would say, 'Thank you. Good-bye.' But sometimes the best thing I could do for him was to reverse my previous advice and sell something we had recently bought. He didn't make that hard for me to do. He didn't rehash all my past mistakes. He never looked back."

My friend happens to be an excellent broker, so he didn't find himself reversing his previous advice very often. While it is important to be flexible and not set your investment portfolio in stone, it is equally important not to set it in quicksand. If you find that your broker is constantly backtracking on previous advice and selling today what you bought last week, or even last year, you should reconsider your affiliation. The best investments are bought and held for the long haul. If your broker fights you on this, you have the wrong broker. If you cannot accept this yourself and are constantly tempted to go for a quick killing, it will be easy to find a broker who will oblige you. Ultimately, we all get the brokers we deserve.

CHAPTER 5

YOUR INVESTMENT
PROGRAM—BASIC CHOICES

The Elusive Perfect Investment

Just so you'll know it in case you ever run across it, this is what
the perfect investment would look like:

1. It pays a guaranteed high dividend or interest rate, at
   least double the current rate of inflation.
2. Your principal (the money you have invested) is absolutely safe. It's guaranteed not only by the United
   States government but also by the combined resources
   of NATO, OPEC, Superman, and Bill Gates.
3. The potential for growth is excellent. Your investment is
   also likely to appreciate in value at double-digit rates.
4. It is perfectly liquid. If you need your money back today
   for any reason, you can have it immediately.
5. All of your earnings are 100 percent tax-free. Every
   penny that you make you get to keep.
6. It does the dishes.

Only kidding about number 6, of course, but your chance
of finding one investment with characteristics 1 through 5
combined is, alas, also just a dream. There is no way it could

be otherwise. If an investment somehow appeared offering characteristics 2 through 5, say, it would immediately be recognized as so desirable that crowds would clamor to buy it, driving up its price so that characteristic 1 would no longer apply. But even the prospect of getting 2 through 5 at the same time is a dream. No investment simultaneously offers characteristics 2 and 3—the potential for growth is always accompanied by the possibility of decline. In investing, you cannot have everything. You cannot square the circle.

You can, however, have something, and it can be precisely the thing that is just right for you. It's not a terribly difficult feat to find investments possessing any one (or even two or three) of our ideal characteristics. You can choose which characteristic is most important to you, and you can get it—even though you will have to accept the trade-off of not getting something else. If you want high current income from an investment, you can get it—if you're willing to sacrifice the chance of it substantially appreciating in value. If you're hoping for appreciation, you'll have to give up some safety. If you insist on safety, you'll have to give up some income and some potential for price appreciation. Every benefit has a price, but it will often be a price that you are willing to pay.

In many cases, deciding what you value most in an investment will be easy. If you are retired or close to it, you will want current income and safety, and you will not care as much about long-term growth potential. If you are young and gainfully employed, however, you will probably have the opposite concerns. If you are in a high tax bracket, then some kind of tax-advantaged investment will appeal to you. If you have a nervous stomach, you will value safety. If you enjoy gambling, then you may have a taste for risky investments. Before you invest in anything, you should sit down with your broker and analyze your needs—both economic and emotional—to determine which investment vehicles are best suited to you.

The table on page 60 lists some kinds of investments and the characteristics they possess. You will note some of the trade-offs involved. No single investment has an X in every row.

You Can't Square the Circle

This table shows the major attractions and trade-offs generally associated with a wide range of investments. As in golf, you've got to reach for the right club if you hope to get the right results. The table assumes you're going to buy and hold your investments and not seek capital appreciation through trading.

Investments	Major Attributes						Other Attributes	
	Income		Growth Potential		Security of Principal			
	High Level	Security of Income	Short-term	Long-term	Secure	At Risk	Liquidity	Tax Advantages
Lending Investments								
U.S. Treasury Securities		x			x		x	x
Federal Agency Securities		x			x		x	z
Certificates of Deposit		x			x		z	
Money Market Funds		x			x		x	z
Corporate Bonds	x	x			z		x	
High-Yield Bonds	x			x		x	x	
Convertible Bonds		x		x	z	x	x	
Municipal Bonds	z	x			z		x	x
Zero Coupon Bonds				x	x		x	z
Mortgage-Backed Securities	x	x			x		x	
International Bonds	z	z		x		z		
Owning Investments								
Preferred Stocks	x	x				z	x	
Common Stock	z	z	z	x		x	x	
Foreign Stocks	z	z		x		x	z	
Real Estate	z	z		x		x		
Gold and Silver				x		x	x	
Collectibles				x		x		
Commodity Futures			x			x		

x = generally applicable
z = depends on specific choices in this category

Your choices are numerous, particularly in today's deregulated investment climate, but don't despair of ever being able to understand, much less weigh, all of your options. To begin with, they all have one element in common: Every investment promises to deliver to you a future flow of cash. You are laying out some money today (your "principal") that you have diverted, probably with some pain, from current consumption; in exchange you are receiving the right to participate in your chosen investment's future cash flow.

The arrangement can be very simple. You buy a federally insured certificate of deposit (CD) from a bank, and you will receive a reliable cash flow of say, 6 percent, in the form of an interest payment every three months for the life of the investment, and then you get your principal back at maturity. Or the arrangement may be more complex. You buy stock in a corporation and receive some cash flow in the form of dividends. You receive additional cash flow (you hope) in the form of capital appreciation if and when the price of the stock goes up. Your dividend cash flow is typically less than you would have received if you had taken the same amount of money and bought a certificate of deposit, but the part of the cash flow from capital appreciation will (you hope) more than make up the difference. If the price of the stock goes down, you will be looking at a cash flow that is less than you would have obtained if you had purchased a CD, which is not likely to make you very happy.

Naturally, you want as large a cash flow as possible in exchange for handing over your principal. This quest will lead you directly to the most basic of all investment trade-offs. The greater the potential cash flow from an investment, the greater the risk that it will not be delivered. You can put your money into a savings account and earn 4 percent a year insured by an agency of the U.S. government. You can put your money into a promising new high tech stock and make 50 percent a year if the stock moves up, or lose 50 percent a year if it moves down. You can put your money on Seabiscuit in the seventh and make 1,000 percent on your investment in a few minutes, unless you lose it all, which is far more likely.

Before people plop down their money for any investment, they size up the risks involved. They will demand a higher rate of return from an investment that appears moderately safe than they will from an investment that appears very safe. That extra return is the reward they expect to receive for accepting additional risk. Proprietors of uncertain ventures seeking investment dollars have no choice but to offer higher rates of return than, say, the United States Treasury.

This risk/reward trade-off not only figures prominently in the choice between investment types but also in selecting particular investments within each category. Consider the choice between buying a corporate bond and investing in a piece of real estate. Corporate bonds may pay 8 percent, as long as the issuing corporation stays solvent. A piece of real estate may appreciate 20 percent a year if yuppies move into the neighborhood, but it may decline 20 percent in value if junkies head them off at the corner. If you buy the real estate, you're taking a chance—and looking at a greater potential cash flow in exchange for your willingness to take that chance.

But what if you decide to buy the corporate bond? There are some that pay interest of 6 percent a year and others that pay 10 percent. Why do you think one is paying more than the other? Do you feel safer lending money to General Electric or to the Let's Hope It Works New Venture Corporation?

How much risk can you *bear* to live with? Surprisingly, the answer to that question does not always depend on how much risk a person can *afford* to live with. There are many very wealthy people who can well afford to take chances but who are emotionally incapable of living with the idea of losing money. There are, on the other hand, people of more moderate means who positively relish taking a flier. You may have some idea where you fit on this spectrum, but people often discover their true feelings about risk only after they've stopped thinking about it in the abstract and have actually put up some money. If after you have begun your investment program, you find that you are kept awake nights worrying about what you might lose, then you have invested too speculatively. The best rule here is: Keep selling until you can sleep comfortably.

"Lending" Investments vs. "Owning" Investments

There are basically two things you can do with your investment money: You can lend it to somebody, or you can buy something with it.

When you put your money in a savings account, you are lending it to the bank, which uses it to make its own loans and investments. When you "buy" a certificate of deposit, you are still lending your money to the bank. When you buy a corporate bond, you are lending your money to the corporation that issued the bond.

When you buy a share of common stock, however, you are buying a piece of the corporation and becoming a co-owner. When you buy real estate, or gold, or soybeans, or a mint-condition Mighty Morphin Power Rangers secret signal ring, you are also becoming an owner of something, not a lender.

As a general rule, lending your money involves less risk than buying an ownership interest in something with it. Therefore, the rate of return you can expect to receive on "lending" investments typically will be lower than the potential rate of return on "owning" investments. It's the old risk/return trade-off.

Many "lending" investments are known as "fixed-income investments," because they provide a reliable and predictable income stream at a predetermined rate. A 6 percent certificate of deposit will pay a steady 6 percent, and it's virtually risk-free. You can plan your family budget around that income, which is nice. But holders of fixed-income investments face another kind of risk. While a 6 percent certificate of deposit will never pay less than 6 percent, neither will it ever pay more—even if the inflation rate should suddenly soar to 15 percent.

In the late 1970s, many people found that they were essentially losing money by owning what had once looked like "risk-free" fixed-income investments. Because the inflation rate was higher than the rate of return on their fixed-income investments, they had less and less purchasing power. In the early 1980s, on the other hand, fixed-income investments fared very well relative to inflation. The inflation rate dropped, but investors were skeptical that it was down for good. Because investors were concerned that inflation would once again rear its ugly head, they sought interest rates on fixed-income investments that reflected past, not present, rates of inflation. By the time it was finally clear that inflation would stay down, many investors had locked in remarkably high "real" interest rates on long-term certificates of deposit and corporate and government bonds. (The "real" interest rate is the difference between an investment's stated interest rate and the rate of inflation.) In the 1990s, many investors were still concerned about inflation, but it generally seemed to be under control, so fixed-income investments did not have to offer investors any extra incentives to attract them.

Historically, fixed-income investments have not performed all that well over the long term. They tend to run about three percentage points ahead of inflation (or ahead of what borrowers and lenders expect inflation to be). In periods of rapidly increasing inflation, they have often fallen behind. Most fixed-income investments have faithfully continued to pay what they promised to pay, and the principal invested in them has generally been safe as well, even if its purchasing power was shrinking. That, of course, assumes that an investor buys and holds a fixed-income investment until it matures. You can buy and sell many of these instruments at any point in their life at whatever prices are prevailing in the market. These prices rise and fall in relation to current interest rates and changes in the perception of the particular instrument. Thus, there is the potential for substantial capital gains, and losses, associated with trading fixed-income instruments. Nonetheless, the instruments themselves have unchanging interest rates.

"Owning" or "equity" investments, on the other hand, provide fewer guarantees. An "owning" investor's cash flow is not protected. The price of a share of stock, or an ounce of gold, or a Digimon trading card, can fall through the floor, endangering principal, to say nothing of interest. (No interest at all is paid on gold or trading cards, and dividends on shares of stock rise and fall with corporate fortunes.) But on the other hand, an "owning" investment's "upside" is unlimited. A corporate bond pays what it pays but a share of stock in that same corporation can soar to many times its original value if the corporation flourishes, and the dividends it pays can be raised again and again.

Some "fixed"-income investments pay variable rates of interest—instead of paying you 5 percent of what you invested, they may pay an amount that is equal to whatever is the prime rate of interest at major banks or whatever U.S. Treasury notes are paying plus 1 percent. Nevertheless, these are fixed-income investments in the sense that the rate of return is predetermined, so you won't get more than was promised to you, unless you succeed in selling them prior to maturity and generating a capital gain. Even if the interest rate is variable, it may not be sufficient to offset the effects of inflation.

"Lending" investments do not offer security against the risk of inflation, while "owning" investments offer the alluring potential of protection against inflation and growth that can exceed the inflation rate. Experience has shown that on average, "owning" or "equity" investments—particularly stocks and real estate—have provided the best long-term investment returns for most people, and I will deal with each of them in subsequent chapters. What I regard as higher-risk and speculative investments will get their own chapter after that. Meanwhile, the rest of this chapter will describe the most common "lending" investments, and a few assorted "owning" ones as well.

We're not only going to look at some things you can invest in, we're also going to look at some of the ways you can make those investments. Those are two different issues. You first need to decide whether you want to own stocks, or bonds, or gold; then you need to decide whether you want to buy these things directly or through a mutual fund, a unit investment trust, or some other kind of collective investment vehicle. Before giving an overview of investments, and examining vehicles for purchasing those investments, however, it is important to understand the concept of market risk involved in "lending" or fixed-income investments.

Market Risk in Fixed-Income Investments

If you own a fixed-income investment, that means you lent money to some person or entity, and they owe you the money. If they owe you $1,000, however, that doesn't mean the value of your investment is always $1,000. You need to understand that although bonds, certificates of deposit, and other fixed-income investments are quoted in terms of a specific "face value," their "market value" at any point in time prior to maturity could be more or less than that. The fact that the market value varies is called "market risk." That's different from the risk that the other party won't pay you back.

Market risk comes into play only if an owner of a fixed-income investment decides to sell it before it matures or comes due. Owners of bonds are free to do that; indeed, that's part of what makes a bond different from a loan. If you paid $1,000 for a twenty-year bond ten years ago, you will receive $1,000 when it matures ten years from now, plus interest every six months. However, that doesn't mean someone will necessarily pay you $1,000 for it at every point in time over the twenty-year period. The amount a prospective buyer will pay for your bond depends on how the interest rate on that bond compares with current interest rates.

Suppose you own a high-quality $1,000 corporate bond paying 6 percent interest ($60 a year) and you decide to sell it at a time when new bond issues of comparable quality are paying 8 percent. Clearly, no one of reasonable intelligence will pay you $1,000 for your bond when they could use that same $1,000 to buy a new bond paying 8 percent. Someone might, however, be willing to pay $750 for your 6 percent bond because the $60 annual interest he or she will receive would be equal to 8 percent of $750. Your bond would thus sell at a discount to reflect the change in interest rates.

The $1,000 principal on your bond may be quite secure; nonetheless, $1,000 is what your bond is worth only if you hold it to maturity. By selling it before maturity, you have subjected yourself to "market risk," and in this case you have lost. But you can also win at this game if interest rates have gone down. For example, a $1,000 8 percent bond will be worth $1,233 if interest rates have fallen to 6 percent.

It's clear that somebody is always deciding that he or she wants to sell bonds before they mature because the investor needs the cash or sees a more attractive investment opportunity elsewhere. But why might someone want to buy these bonds? First of all, a "used bond" is still a reliable investment, and it's paying current interest rates. (It's paying current rates because its selling price is adjusted so that its interest payments work out to be equal to current rates for similar bonds.) Meanwhile, there's always a chance that interest rates will go down, which means that the value of your bond will go up, and you can sell it at a profit instead of just collecting interest and waiting for it to mature. When the bond reaches its maturity, the issuer will pay you its full face value, no matter what you paid for it. Thus, you can pay less than $1,000 for a bond that will pay you $1,000 when it matures in two years—but, alas, this apparent bonanza is figured into the market price of the bond, and you'll still end up with a return about equal to what other bond investors are earning.

Perhaps you like the idea of bonds as a way of saving for a particular purchase or event, but you don't want to get caught up in market risk by having to sell your bonds when it's time to make your purchase. You could look for newly issued bonds that mature when it's time to make your purchase—if that purchase is scheduled twenty years hence. It's probably easier to find and buy already issued bonds in the secondary market that are due to mature exactly when you're going to need your money back (for example, the year your son or daughter goes to college).

Now that you understand the way the market values of fixed-income investments move, let's look at some of the categories of those investments that you might want to own.

U.S. Treasury Securities

We're talking safety here. These are direct obligations of the United States government, which, if all else fails, can always tax somebody to raise the money to pay them off. In the U.S. and around the world, Treasury securities are the gold standard of safety. It's difficult to imagine the Treasury being unable to make good on its obligations. If you can imagine circumstances in which it can't pay, those circumstances probably involve a state of global chaos in which other institutions are even less likely to be able to meet their financial obligations. Treasury securities come in several flavors:

Treasury bills: These are issued in minimum denominations of $1,000 and mature in a year or less. They bear no stated interest rates; instead, they're sold at auction for less than their face (or "par") value. When they come due, their full par value is paid out. For example, you might pay $992 for a T-bill and receive $1,000 when it matures three months later.

Treasury notes: These are issued in minimums of $1,000 and mature in two to ten years. They carry stated interest rates and pay interest semiannually. Treasury notes are sold through auctions and may be bought for less or more than face value, depending upon whether the bidders considered the stated interest rate to be a good deal or not.

Treasury bonds: These are like notes in every way, except they mature in more than ten years.

Because Treasury securities are considered risk-free, they do not pay high interest rates (it's the old risk/return trade-off). You can buy them at auction directly from the federal government, which involves some paperwork, or from a stock-broker or bank, which involves a fee.

Probably the best-known Treasury securities are United States savings bonds, which many people remember from childhood school savings plans. Savings bonds fell out of favor for a while because the interest rates they offered were substantially below market rates. Today's savings bonds, however, are a better deal than they were in the past. Their interest rate is adjusted every six months (to 90 percent of the average five-year Treasury securities yields). Savings bonds are sold at a discount from their face value, like zero coupon bonds (which are described later). Unlike most other zero coupon bonds, however, no federal income tax is due on interest earned until the bonds are cashed in. Moreover, the interest they pay, like that on other U.S. government securities, is exempt from state and local income taxes.

In addition to securities issued by the U.S. Treasury, there are a variety of securities issued by various U.S. government agencies, like the Federal Home Loan Bank System and government-sponsored enterprises such as Fannie Mae (formerly the Federal National Mortgage Association). These securities are a step removed from the federal government itself, but they are still considered to be very safe.

Once they are issued, Treasury and agency securities trade on the secondary market, and they can be bought and sold at market prices through a broker.

Certificates of Deposit (CDs)

We're still talking safety here. CDs are usually issued by commercial banks, savings banks, and savings and loan associations.

They're sold by these institutions and by brokerage firms as well. CDs pay a reliable, fixed rate of interest over a specified period of time. The principal and interest is often insured up to $100,000 by an agency of the U.S. government. The interest rates offered to those who sign up for a new CD vary from week to week, depending on the issuer's guess about which way other interest rates are going. If your guess is that interest rates are on the way down, then buying a long-term CD is a safe way to lock in today's higher rate. If your guess is wrong, however, you will be stuck with a below-market rate until your CD matures.

The longer the term of the CD you buy, the higher the rate you will get. This is a consequence of the risk/return trade-off. Tying up your money for two years is riskier than tying it up for one year because there is more time for interest rates to rise and make your CD look like a bad deal; you are rewarded for accepting the longer term with a slightly higher interest rate.

If you want to cash in your CD early, either to put your money into a better investment or to cover emergency expenses, you will have to pay a penalty. If you bought your CD through a broker, you can sell it in the secondary market without an early-withdrawal penalty. But sellers in the secondary market are exposed to "market risk," so you could be offered less (or more) than the face amount of the CD.

While CDs are generally issued at fixed rates, there have been some variable-rate CDs. These typically offer an interest rate that is less than what is available on fixed rates, but offer the potential to go above that rate if some benchmark rate or indicator goes up. Once again, it's the risk/reward trade-off.

Corporate Bonds

To finance their operations, corporations are always borrowing money. Often they borrow from banks, but much of the money companies need is borrowed from the general public through the issuance of corporate bonds. These bonds generally pay a fixed interest rate over a fixed period of time. Bonds may have a maturity of ten, twenty, or even thirty years. Interest payments are usually made to the bondholders every six months. At maturity, the bondholders' principal is returned.

The interest rates paid on corporate bonds vary according to the maturity of the bonds (the longer the term, the higher the rate) and according to the creditworthiness of the issuing corporation. If you are considering buying bonds, you don't have to investigate a corporation's finances yourself; several firms, including Standard & Poor's and Moody's Investors Service, issue widely used letter grades representing their assessment of the bond issuer's ability to meet its obligations. You've probably seen reference to these ratings, which range from AAA, the highest-quality ranking, down to AA and A and then to BBB, BB, B, and so on down to C.

These ratings are by no means perfect, but they allow you to make quick comparisons between corporate bonds in terms of quality and returns. Bonds that are rated A should be paying more interest than those rated AA; otherwise, investors would gravitate to the AA bonds because they would be able to get the same return as the A-rated bonds with less risk.

Another factor affecting the interest rate on a particular issue is whether the bond is backed by specific assets of the corporation (which decreases the bond buyer's risk) or is a "debenture," backed only by the company's general credit and good name. If someone owes you money and doesn't pay, it's easier to collect by foreclosing on a building or a truck and selling it at auction than it is to raise money from a general claim on the company.

Corporate bonds usually pay higher rates than short-term investments, like money market funds, or longer-term Treasury securities or certificates of deposit. They can be an excellent way of locking in high interest rates. (Some long-term high-quality bonds paid as much as 18 percent to those lucky investors who bought them in 1981 and held on to them as rates fell sharply.) There is, however, a catch to this business of locking in high rates. The fine print on many bonds specifies that they can be "called," or redeemed, before maturity. If a corporation issues a twenty-year bond paying, say, 10 percent and a few years later the interest rate on comparable new issues has fallen to 8 percent, that corporation will be a little glum about the prospect of paying above-market interest rates for the next eighteen years. If the bond issue is callable, the corporation has the right to redeem the bonds at face value (or, sometimes, at a premium), say thank you to the nice bondholders for lending their money for two years at 10 percent, and promptly issue new 8 percent bonds to replace the money it just paid out when it called the old 10 percent bonds. (The company would be happy to sell those 8 percent bonds to the former holders of the 10 percent bonds; those individuals, however, may be less than happy about the whole situation.)

As will be noted later, corporate bonds can be purchased directly by an investor, or they can be bought through mutual funds, unit investment trusts, and other vehicles that bring together groups of investors to pool their funds and buy groups of securities.

"High-Yield" or "Junk" Bonds

So-called high-yield bonds are simply a relatively high-risk version of corporate bonds. Technically, "high-yield bonds," or "junk bonds," as their detractors used to call them, are bonds that have received a rating below "investment grade" by the credit-rating agencies, and consequently they have to offer a relatively high interest rate to induce investors to buy them. These bonds may be used by companies with very high levels of debt or poor track records in revenue growth or profits. Or they may be issued by new companies that don't have much of a track record at all. During the 1980s, many issuers of junk bonds were firms involved in "leveraged buyouts." (In a leveraged buyout, or LBO, a group of investors or corporate managers buys all the outstanding shares of stock in a corporation. It's called leveraged because they buy the company by using money borrowed from the public by issuing junk bonds.)

For one reason or another, high-yield bonds entail a significant risk that the issuing companies will not be able to keep up the interest payments, so they offer yields considerably higher than those on more secure investment-grade corporate bonds. One way to reduce the risk inherent in investing in high-yield bonds is to buy those of several different issuers, or to invest in a mutual fund that buys high-yield bonds. Investing in many different issues provides some reduction in the risk of default associated with these securities. They can't all default at once, can they?

Convertible Bonds

Another special category of corporate bonds consists of "convertible" issues. These are bonds that can be exchanged for a specified number of shares of the issuing corporation's common stock. Convertible bondholders thus share in the growth potential offered by stock (if the price of a company's stock goes up, the value of bonds that may be exchanged for that stock naturally increases too), yet investors still enjoy the relative security and stable interest rates of a bond. Sounds like you can have your cake and eat it too? Not quite. Because convertibles offer certain advantages, they generally pay lower interest rates than nonconvertible bonds of equal credit quality.

Municipal Bonds

These are bonds that are issued not by corporations but rather by the government of cities and states, and by agencies of these local governments. Examples of those issuing "muni bonds" would not only include the State of Wisconsin or the City of Denver, but also the Port Authority of New York and New Jersey and thousands of local school boards and airport authorities. As with corporate bonds, the creditworthiness of the issuers is graded by bond-rating services, and interest rates vary according to those ratings and the length of term. Many municipals are callable before their stated maturity.

The great appeal of municipal bonds is that the interest they earn is free of federal income tax. (They are also generally free of state and local income taxes when purchased by residents of the states in which they are issued.) This makes municipal bonds extremely attractive to investors in the higher tax brackets. To an investor in the 28 percent bracket, a municipal bond paying 5 percent is worth exactly as much as a corporate bond paying nearly 7 percent. Municipal bond issuers are therefore able to sell their bonds at lower interest rates than corporations. You'll have to sit down and work out your own tax situation to decide if a particular municipal bond is a good buy for you.

But bear in mind that municipal bonds are inevitably a bad choice for 401(k) plans and other tax-deferred investment vehicles. Why accept a lower interest rate in exchange for a tax-free return when any bonds you buy for your 401(k) are automatically exempt from taxation until you withdraw the funds? Moreover, the money you withdraw from your 401(k) will be taxed, even if it is derived from municipal bonds.

Zero Coupon Bonds

A fair amount of attention has been devoted to zero coupon bonds in recent years, although there is nothing terribly new about them. U.S. savings bonds have always been a form of zero coupon bond. That is, they do not make periodic interest payments to those who own them. Instead, they are issued at a discount from their face value, and when they mature, the owners are given the full face value. In effect, you get all your interest at the end, in one lump sum.

Zero coupon bonds get their name from the fact that traditional bonds used to come with a set of coupons attached. You clipped one off every six months and turned it in to receive your interest payment. While a traditional twenty-year, 7 percent, $1,000 bond will cost you $1,000 and provide you with a check for $35 every six months, a twenty-year, 7 percent, $1,000 "zero" might cost you about $250 and pay you nothing for twenty years. Then it will pay you $1,000 at maturity.

Turning $250 into $1,000 sounds like a pretty good deal, doesn't it? But it's just one more demonstration of the remarkable powers of compound interest. And it's directly related to the one great advantage of zero coupon bonds. Unlike coupon bonds, zeros guarantee not only to pay you the specified interest rate on your principal; they also guarantee to pay the same rate of interest on your interest. To understand why this is important, consider what would happen if you bought a traditional 7 percent $1,000 bond and interest rates then fell to 5 percent. You'd get your 7 percent interest on the bond, all right, in the form of $35 every six months. But what kind of return would you get if you proceeded to reinvest that $35? Only 5 percent.

If you had bought the zero coupon bond instead, your $35 in interest would be automatically reinvested at 7 percent, no matter what the current interest rate was. Zero coupon bonds are thus the best possible way to lock in high interest rates far into the future. The flip side of this—and there's always a flip side, isn't there?—is that if interest rates go up after you buy your bond, you are locked into receiving what is now a below-market interest rate on your interest payments instead of being able to receive and reinvest them at higher rates. And if you want to sell your bond, nobody is going to pay you very much for it.

Zero coupon bonds are issued primarily by the U.S. Treasury and federal agencies, and to a lesser extent by municipalities and corporations. In addition, several brokerage houses have created their own zero coupon issues based on various federal government securities.

If you decide to invest in zeros, you should keep in mind that some issues can be called early, not at their face value but according to a graduated redemption schedule. And note also that although no annual interest payments are made to you, the Internal Revenue Service will tax you as if they were (except for tax-free municipal zero coupon bonds). Thus, you're paying taxes on money that you have earned on paper but haven't actually received yet. You might therefore want to consider taxable zero coupon bonds only for your tax-deferred retirement plans.

Mortgage-Backed Securities

Mortgages are generally nice safe investments for lenders. When individuals fall on hard times, they may stiff the local department stores and not pay their credit card bills, but they'll keep making their mortgage payments as long as they can. After all, they need a place to sleep. It used to be that only banks, savings and loan associations, and other institutions owned mortgage loans. These entities lent money to homeowners and then sat back for thirty years while the borrowers (in most cases) reliably repaid them.

Today, you too can be a mortgage lender by investing in mortgage-backed securities. The best-known of these are "Ginnie Maes," issued by the Government National Mortgage Association (GNMA). GNMA buys federally insured mortgages from banks and other lending institutions, puts them together into pools consisting of thousands of mortgages, and then sells shares in those pools. Each of these investors receives a proportionate share of the principal and interest payments made on those mortgages. The smallest unit sold by GNMA costs $25,000, but investors may buy into GNMAs indirectly by putting as little as $1,000 or so into a GNMA mutual fund or unit trust.

Ginnie Maes are very safe, not only because most people make their mortgage payments but also because they are guaranteed by the U.S. government. And they also pay relatively high interest rates. Aha, you say, at last an exception to the risk/return trade-off. Not so fast. There are two additional wrinkles associated with mortgage-backed securities.

First of all, Ginnie Maes are "self-liquidating." They're pass-through securities in which every month, Ginnie Maes give the securities holders their share of the principal and interest payments the homeowners have made on their mortgages. If interest rates are falling, it will be difficult to reinvest that returned principal and interest at as high a rate as the Ginnie Mae is paying. Second, if home mortgage rates are declining, some of the people whose home mortgages make up the Ginnie Mae pool may decide to pay off their mortgages ahead of schedule. Some will refinance their houses with new mortgages issued at the lower current rates. Others will capitalize on the lower rates by trading up to a bigger house. In either case, a decline in interest rates means an increase in mortgage prepayments. Thus, Ginnie Mae holders face a double whammy: When rates decline, they get more of their investment back just when there are only lower rate alternatives for reinvesting it.

Mortgage-backed securities similar to Ginnie Maes are also sold by Freddie Mac (formerly the Federal Home Loan Mortgage Corporation) and Fannie Mae. Some privately packaged mortgage-backed securities are also available.

Many investors were wary of mortgage-backed securities because they never knew how many homeowners would prepay their mortgages, leaving the investors with cash that they had to re-invest. The response crafted in the 1980s was the "collateralized mortgage obligation" (CMO). CMOs are bonds backed by mortgages, but they are more predictable than Ginnie Maes. Basically, the flow of mortgage payments are divided up into separate classes, making it possible to use the same pool of mortgages to issue several sets of bonds with targeted maturities. Investors in various classes of a CMO can each count on receiving payments until a specified date with less uncertainty regarding cash flow and less "market risk" than is associated with traditional Ginnies, Fannies, or Freddies. While CMOs helped reduce some of the uncertainty associated with the rate at which investors in mortgage-backed securities got their money back, CMOs introduced a variety of other risks. Indeed, some of the classes of a CMO presented highly uncertain payment flows and changes in maturity.

The dramatic growth in the mortgage-backed securities marketplace has led to the creation of a variety of other asset-backed securities. You can buy bonds that are backed by money that will be paid to credit cards, money paid by those who have auto loans, and a wide assortment of other cash flows. Asset-backed securities, though often of good quality, are at least mildly exotic securities, so they bear close examination.

International Bonds

Foreign issuers have been coming to the U.S. bond market for decades because it is the largest and most liquid fixed-income market in the world. You can easily buy bonds issued in this country by foreign governments and corporations. In order to be sold to the public in the U.S., these bonds have to meet the same regulatory requirements as domestic issues, and all interest payments and transactions are denominated in U.S. dollars. They're typically rated for creditworthiness by the rating agencies.

However, as technology has made the world a smaller place, it has become increasingly easy to buy bonds issued by foreign governments and foreign companies in markets outside the U.S. With a call to your broker, you can buy Swiss government bonds, denominated in Swiss francs, in Zurich. Or you can buy Siemens bonds, denominated in euros, in Germany.

In many cases, foreign bonds pay far higher interest rates

than anything offered in the U.S. market. The problem is exchange rates. You can buy a bond abroad that pays 12 percent, while you can only get bonds paying 8 percent in the U.S. But when you convert your pounds or euros into dollars, this may either substantially erode your return or substantially enlarge it. For most people, buying foreign bonds is not unlike buying a pile of euros or yen, putting them in a drawer for a few years, and then taking them out and exchanging them for dollars. It may be a good investment, or it may not, but it's probably too complicated for mere mortals.

Debt vs. Equity Investments

The vast fixed-income market is composed of a seemingly endless array of investments. They come in every maturity, they're backed by everything imaginable (from general promises to pay to a specific Boeing 747 identifiable by the serial number on its wing), and they pay interest on all kinds of schedules and in a variety of forms. What they all have in common is that they are lending investments.

However, many people want and need "owning" investments. We'll get to shares of stock and real estate in the next two chapters. Meanwhile, you too can be the proud "owner" of some of the following:

Preferred Stocks

What most people think of as stock is common stock, and that's the subject of the next chapter. But there is also preferred stock, which looks like stock but acts like a bond. Like bonds, preferred shares are issued with a designated "par value" and they often have a specified dividend. Corporations are obligated to pay preferred stock dividends before any dividends are paid to holders of common stock (but after interest payments have been made on corporate bonds), so preferred stockholders get "preferred" treatment. Similarly, if a company goes broke, the claims of the preferred stock owners are satisfied after those of creditors (who include bondholders) but before the owners of common stock. Moreover, many preferred stock issues are "cumulative," which means that if dividends are skipped any year (or years), all dividends, past and present, must be paid in full before any common stock dividends can be paid. Some preferred stock is also "convertible" into shares of common stock anytime the shareholder pleases.

Corporations enjoy certain tax benefits from owning the preferred stock of other corporations. Consequently, corporations bid up the price of preferred stock to reflect those benefits. This makes many preferred stocks a noncompetitive investment for individuals.

In recent years, the market for preferred stock has been significantly transformed by the creation of new instruments. Fixed-rate capital (FRC) securities constituted virtually all of the new preferred stock issues brought to market in the mid-1990s. These instruments are specifically designed for individual investors. While traditional preferred shares are senior equity securities, FRCs are technically fixed-income instruments issued by major corporations, insurance companies, and such entities as the Tennessee Valley Authority. There has been a proliferation of such instruments with an alphabet soup of names, including MIPs and QUIDs, and these have transformed the once-staid world of preferred stock.

Gold and Silver

Precious metals are popular investments in some circles, especially during periods of high inflation, because, like other commodities, they tend to increase in value along with the inflation rate. They are, after all, things, and an increase in the price of things is the definition of inflation.

Gold has special characteristics, however, that set it apart from other commodities. It has a long heritage of use as money, possessing ideal traits for the role: It is scarce, transportable, nonperishable, and divisible. It is also highly liquid and easily sold at current market prices anywhere in the world. If you're going to flee the country and don't know where you're going, your prospects in your new home, wherever it is, will probably be a lot better if you arrive with a briefcase full of gold coins than with a briefcase full of stock certificates and bank accounts from a country in the midst of a revolution. That's why gold has traditionally been used to store wealth by people living in societies suffering economic or political instability.

Many investors in gold are essentially betting on calamity. Despite that, or because of it, many investors like to keep at least a small share of their assets in gold, silver (which is really an industrial metal, and is less valuable than gold), or other precious metals. There are several ways to invest in gold:

- Gold bullion bars
- Gold bullion coins issued by the United States, South Africa, Canada, China, and other countries
- Stock in gold-mining companies or mutual funds that invest in these companies
- Precious metals mutual funds or managed portfolios
- Gold futures (for a description of futures, see Chapter 10)

The main drawback of owning actual gold, in the form of bullion or coins, is that the stuff just sits there. It doesn't create wealth or give you a share in the creation of wealth, and it doesn't earn interest or pay dividends. In fact, it costs you money for storage and insurance. It's great to have in a period of hyperinflation or a revolution. But if the Four Horsemen of the Apocalypse don't ride through your town, your investment in gold has kept you from the gains you could have had investing in other things.

Collectibles

Collectibles, which include antiques, paintings, rare coins and stamps, and even back-issue comic books, are another popular investment during inflationary times. The prices of some of these items have sometimes soared out of sight. A van Gogh painting of a vase of sunflowers sold at auction for $39.9 million. A 1910 baseball card depicting Honus Wagner, who played shortstop for the Pittsburgh Pirates, sold at auction for $451,000 in 1991 and was resold for $580,000 in 1996. And a bat used by Babe Ruth was sold for $63,000 in 1994. In 1996, a widely publicized auction of items belonging to Jacqueline Kennedy Onassis fetched such prices as $211,500 for a necklace of simulated pearls, $48,875 for a silver-cased tape measure, and $27,600 for a set of ashtrays.

But collectibles are an especially tricky investment because of the size of the "spread," which is the gap between the net buying price and the net selling price of a thing. If gold is currently going for $300 an ounce, you can buy an ounce for $300 (plus several dollars for a dealer's commission) or you can sell an ounce for $300 (minus a few dollars for a dealer's commission). Either way, your net price will be pretty close to $300. The spread is small.

Collectibles don't work that way. Most collectibles are sold in retail stores, whose proprietors expect, and get, a conventional retail markup on their merchandise. An antique spinning wheel that a dealer is selling for $400 may have cost the dealer only $200. If you buy that spinning wheel for $400, and the value of antiques proceeds to increase a full 100 percent, that same dealer will be happy to buy the spinning wheel back from you—for $400. Prices have to double for you to break even.

The spreads in all collectibles are not this wide, and they can be reduced by buying and selling at auctions and in private sales. But collectibles are still a tough area in which to realize a profit.

This is partly because the market for many collectibles

is a "thin" one, with far fewer people standing ready to buy and sell than there are in markets for stocks and bonds. You can always find a thousand people interested in buying your shares of Xerox. You can't be sure of finding a crowd interested in your collection of Rudolph Valentino autographs.

With that in mind, go right out and buy modern American art, or Icelandic commemoratives, or rare first editions of Batman comic books. But buy only things that you enjoy owning, because the psychic rewards you get from having your collectibles in your living room may be the only rewards you'll ever see from them. If they do appreciate, consider it a bonus—not an entitlement.

International Investing

International stocks are another investment that you need to consider. Now that may surprise some Americans. After all, it was not very long ago that the U.S. economy was pretty self-contained: We produced all the cars and steel we required, and we grew all the wheat and corn we ate. About all we seemed to look for outside our borders was a little Belgian chocolate, French wine and German scissors! But that was then. For the past few decades, this country has been caught up in rapid global expansion that has not only transformed the U.S. economy but also U.S. investing.

More and more American companies have been generating large portions of their revenues and profits abroad. These days, American icons such as Coca Cola and McDonald's generate about half their sales abroad. And more and more foreign companies have become deeply involved in the United States. As a result of extensive international investment in this country, such all-American names as 7UP, Fox TV, and Ben & Jerry's ice cream are now, in fact, subsidiaries of non-U.S. companies.

As the global economy has expanded, American investors

have gained a new appreciation for markets outside the United States. For years, many Americans thought about international markets just as they thought about foreign travel. You could go to Florida for sunshine and Colorado for skiing, so why think of going anywhere else? And you could invest in just about every kind of industry in our stock market, so why look elsewhere? Well, as the era of global trade and investment unfolded, Americans began to notice that there was a wide world of investments outside the U.S. and no real reason why their portfolios should be confined to the domestic market.

In 1970, the U.S. accounted for 66 percent of global stock market capitalization, but that figure had fallen to less than 50 percent by 1999. That meant many American investors were missing out on more than half of the opportunities available from equities. Not only was there a wider investing landscape out there, many of these markets often performed better than the U.S. market did.

But wait a minute, you might say; in the second half of the 1990s, the S&P 500 advanced more than 20 percent annually, so who needs markets outside the United States? While the U.S. market certainly did outperform non-U.S. markets as a whole over this period (as measured by Morgan Stanley Capital International's Europe, Australasia and Far East Index, better known as EAFE), its 20-percent-plus annual gains pale in comparison to the returns turned in by individual international markets: In 1999, for example, Malaysian stocks surged more than 100 percent, according to MSCI, just as South Korean and Finnish equities did in 1998 and Russian and Turkish stocks did in 1997.

The U.S. was not the top-performing stock market in the world during the 30-year period from 1970 through 2000. In fact, the U.S. was among the world's top three performers only two times during the 1990s. So the key to taking advantage of international investing is to choose carefully, drawing upon the extensive research on international markets now available from several global financial services firms and other sources.

Academic studies have shown that international markets not only offer opportunities for attractive returns, they also help smooth out fluctuations in the overall value of a portfolio. International markets don't move in lock step with the U.S. market. So when markets in the United States are declining, some markets may be rising (and, of course, vice versa). The result is lower overall volatility in the value of your portfolio. And as we've noted, you end up climbing higher when you don't have to dig yourself out of deep holes along the way.

The combination of potentially higher returns and diversification have led many investment advisors to suggest that individuals who are suited for international investing put five to ten percent, or even more, of their investments in non-U.S. companies. If that resonates with you, you can analyze, select, and invest in major companies around the world just as easily and in pretty much the same way as you would invest in U.S. companies. It may be wise to consult a professional financial advisor who can help guide you in this process.

Today, one of the easiest and most popular ways to invest in companies outside the United States is through American Depositary Receipts (ADRs), which have been available since Morgan Stanley introduced them in 1927. ADRs are essentially receipts for shares of stock in foreign companies. The shares are deposited in a bank, and the receipts are bought and sold. The advantage is that these receipts are denominated in dollars instead of the home country currency of the issuing company. Moreover, ADRs can be listed on U.S. stock exchanges, and transactions in them are governed by U.S. laws.

It has also become increasingly simple to buy actual shares of non-U.S. companies. As interest in international investing has grown, many brokerage firms now provide extensive research on non-U.S. markets and companies. U.S. securities firms have joined stock exchanges in other countries and opened offices in cities around the world. Moreover, securities firms abroad have increased their presence here in the United States, opening offices or acquiring U.S.-based brokerage firms.

If you're not ready to jump right in and purchase individual non-U.S. stocks, you may want to consider global or international mutual funds, which offer convenience and professional management and may be a little less risky than purchasing individual international stocks. A "global" fund invests in a portfolio that is composed of investments from both U.S. and non-U.S. companies, while an international mutual fund invests exclusively in stocks of companies outside the United States—so you can match the fund to your needs and level of comfort with international investments. You can even choose mutual funds that specialize in specific regions of the world, or particular countries, which gives you any number of ways to help complement and diversify your domestic portfolio.

For many Americans, international investing has been focused on the advanced industrialized nations of Western Europe, plus Japan. More recently, however, there has been growing interest in the emerging markets. Some of the best-performing stocks in the world are in the rapidly growing countries throughout Asia and Latin America. But this stuff is *definitely* too dicey to invest in, right? It's true, there are special risks associated with investments in emerging markets. But remember, about 120 years ago there was an emerging market that had recently concluded a bloody civil war and had suffered through a financial panic, but was beginning to industrialize. That country was the United States of America, and if your great-great-grandparents had invested in the railroads and manufacturers that were just getting started in the 1880s, you'd be out feeding the polo ponies right now.

New markets are always emerging. There are always nations poised for growth spurts, spurts that will push up their stock markets at a geometric pace. Will the next one be South

Africa or the Czech Republic or Argentina, or will it be some other country? If you get it right, you can make a bundle.

Improvements in stock markets around the world, as well as the international expansion of securities firms, have largely eliminated the risk that transactions in foreign stocks will not be successfully consummated. But keep in mind that international stocks continue to involve foreign exchange risks: no matter how the stock performs, you also have the issue of how the currency in which it was denominated is faring against the U.S. dollar. Fluctuating currency exchange rates can work for or against you. Another type of risk to consider is country risk—the effects of changing political and regulatory environments, as well as overall economic factors. These risks are often magnified in emerging markets, since these countries often have less stable political environments and less established markets and economies. Because of the risks involved, international investing should not be considered a complete investment program but rather as part of an overall plan that includes a variety of asset classes.

Nevertheless, the international dimensions of economic life are looming larger and larger. They influence our daily lives in many ways that are sometimes obvious but usually subtle. And they probably should affect your investing as well. As an investor, it makes sense to own the best companies in the world, regardless of their nationalities. And international diversification can help reduce your overall portfolio risk while offering the potential to increase investment returns.

Choosing Investment Vehicles

So far, we've been talking about things you can invest in, but you also need to address the question of how you're going to invest in those things. In many cases, you can invest directly: After analyzing various alternatives, either on your own or with the help of a broker, you can go out and buy some of the items discussed so far. You can call up a broker and buy some stocks and bonds, for example. Or you can go to a commercial bank or a broker and buy some T-bills. Or you can attend an auction and buy a painting. You might even visit a hobby store and buy some baseball cards.

But there are other ways of investing, and you need to be aware of them. In addition to buying debt or equity investments directly, you may want to consider turning to intermediaries to select and manage them for you. These intermediating vehicles include mutual funds, unit investment trusts, and annuities. (In addition, you might also hire an investment manager to choose your investments for you.) Investing through these vehicles may be seen as investments in some respects—they are often accompanied by prospectuses and subject to rules like the investments we've just been describing. But in other respects, these are not investments but ways of making investments. A mutual fund, for example, is a way in which individual investors can pool their money and jointly invest. This collective approach to investing can and has been used to invest in a wide range of instruments, from stocks and bonds to pork bellies and soybean futures. Here's a look at some of the most common vehicles for investing:

Mutual Funds

Mutual funds are investment pools that sell shares to investors and use the money to buy and maintain a portfolio of investments. Each investor owns a share in the group of investments, and those shares can be bought and sold. Most mutual funds are "open-end" funds, which means they will create and sell new shares to anyone who wants them and buy back the shares from any investor who wants to get out. The trading price is the net asset value, or the market value of the fund's investments divided by the number of shares. Mutual funds usually require a minimum investment of $1,000, though some will let you start with $250 or even $100.

There are mutual funds that invest in virtually any asset

or investment that an individual could buy directly. Money market funds invest in short-term instruments, and other mutual funds invest in stocks, bonds, and assorted other things. The first mutual funds were started in the 1920s, but they really came into their own in the last couple of decades. Many households became investors in mutual funds because that was the form of investment offered through the 401(k) plan provided by their employer.

By the mid-1990s, there were between 7,000 and 10,000 mutual funds registered in the United States. (It depends on whether you're counting organization structures or portfolios of investments.) In any case, there are more funds than there are stocks listed on the New York Stock Exchange. There are funds that specialize in every investment known to Western civilization and every investment technique imaginable.

Why do millions of Americans put money into mutual funds? Mutual funds offer several attractions:

Diversification: Everybody knows you shouldn't put all your eggs in one basket. If you're starting out as an investor, however, you probably can't buy a portfolio of securities all at once. You may buy several different stocks and bonds, but you can't have a fully diversified portfolio on day one. With a mutual fund, however, you can achieve instant diversification. You invest your money, and boom, you own your share of a portfolio of fifty different stocks, or a portfolio of stocks and bonds, or shares in dozens of foreign companies.

Professional management: Mutual funds not only provide a portfolio, they continually manage it, selling some securities and replacing them with others that the managers think offer better opportunities. You might be able to study the market for a few minutes a day. A mutual fund has a full-time staff of professionals who spend their days analyzing investments.

Access: Mutual funds enable small investors to get a piece of investment instruments that they couldn't afford to buy directly. Can't ante up $25,000 to buy a Ginnie Mae mortgage-backed security or $100,000 to buy commercial paper (un-secured short-term IOUs from corporations)? Not to worry. For $1,000 you can get into a mutual fund that buys these instruments.

Convenience: Mutual funds take care of most of your investment bookkeeping for you and happily arrange for you to make automatic investments from your checking account or to reinvest your dividends. They tally your dividend and interest income and your capital gains for tax purposes, and even send out the forms you need to maintain an Individual Retirement Account (IRA).

For taking care of business, mutual funds charge a small annual management fee. This compensates the management company for running the fund. Mutual funds are sold by brokers or other financial services companies as well as through the mail and via toll-free 800 numbers. Some funds impose a sales charge, which may be as high as 8.5 percent of the money you invest. This "load," which goes to compensate the individual and firm selling you the fund, may be imposed at the time of purchase (that's "front-end load") or when you sell your shares ("back-end load"). Other funds are "no-load" funds, which carry no sales charge.

Closed-End Funds

While most mutual funds are "open-end" funds, which issue new shares when investors want to come into the fund and redeem shares from investors who want to get out, there are also closed-end funds. These are like industrial corporations in that they issue a specific number of shares, and new investors can only get into the fund by buying shares from existing investors. The price of shares in closed-end funds reflects not only the net asset value of the fund's investments but also the supply and demand for shares in the fund. Thus, investing in closed-end funds is more complicated than investing in open-end funds. Why bother? As usual, those who make the effort, and get it right, can earn more attractive returns.

Unit Investment Trusts

Unit investment trusts are similar to mutual funds in that they contain portfolios of securities assembled by financial professionals. Shares, or units, in these portfolios can then be purchased by the public. In contrast to most mutual fund portfolios, which are continually adjusted, a unit trust portfolio generally is not expected to change for the life of the trust once the securities are selected.

Unit trusts are assembled with a particular investment goal in mind and generally consist of either stocks, municipal bonds, corporate bonds or government securities. Most equity trusts have a life of about one year; fixed-income unit trusts may have lives of anywhere from five to 30 years. Like mutual funds, unit trusts help to provide diversification, along with accessibility and convenience. And like many mutual funds, investors will generally pay a sales charge when they invest.

The *buy-and-hold* strategy employed by unit trusts suits investors who want to know what they own and who like portfolios that will not change with constant investment activity.

Annuities

Annuities, which are created by insurance companies and marketed by insurance companies and securities brokers, have become increasingly popular because they offer some of the same great tax advantages of 401(k) plans and other retirement plans. And in contrast to these alternatives, there is no annual limit on the amount you can put into an annuity. You can buy an annuity with a single lump-sum payment or with a series of payments spread out over time. And you have your choice of two kinds of annuities: fixed or variable.

In a fixed annuity, the money you deposit is invested as the insurance company sees fit, and the company guarantees to pay into your account a specified "fixed" rate of return for a specified period of time. (The insurance company is taking the risk that it can earn enough from investing your money to pay you what it promised and keep a little for itself.) With a variable annuity, on the other hand, you tell the company how you want your money invested and you get whatever return that pool of money earns. Generally, you are offered a choice of stock, bond, and money market portfolios. You are often allowed to switch freely (and without paying taxes) from one portfolio to another. The rate of return your annuity earns will vary depending on the success (and the relative risk) of the investments you choose. Basically, you get what the pool of money earns. In the event of death, the annuity pays a death benefit, guaranteeing that your beneficiaries will receive a sum that at least equals your original investment.

With either a fixed or a variable annuity, the money in your account compounds tax-deferred as long as you leave it there. As we have seen, that means it will grow at a far healthier rate than an ordinary, taxed investment. If you put $20,000 into an annuity earning 8 percent annually, at the end of twenty years you will have $93,219. If you had put the same $20,000 into a non-tax-deferred investment also paying 8 percent, you would have only $61,300 at the end of the same period (assuming you are in the 28 percent tax bracket). Taxes will be payable on your annuity income when you withdraw it, but the benefit of years of tax-deferred compounding will still leave you ahead. If you're in the 28 percent tax bracket and you withdraw your entire annuity in one lump sum, your tax bill will be $20,501 (that's 28 percent of the $73,219 that your investments earned; you paid tax on your $20,000 in principal before you put it in, so there's no tax on it when you take it out). After taxes, the annuity will leave you with $72,718, or $11,418 more than the non-tax-deferred investment.

In fact, you will probably do better than that, because by

the time you retire you may be in a lower tax bracket. And you are unlikely, in any case, to withdraw your annuity all at once. The majority of annuities are paid out in fixed monthly payments beginning sometime after retirement age. You can generally choose when they begin. You can also choose how long you want the payments to run: until you die; until you and your spouse both die; for a specified number of years or until you die, whichever is longer; or simply for a specified number of years. (If your annuity payments outlive you, they will go to your heirs.) The size of the monthly payout naturally varies depending on the option you choose; longer payout periods pay less each month than shorter ones. Most people choose one of the options that guarantees them a monthly income for the rest of their lives.

Annuities are most appropriate for someone thinking ahead to retirement, since there are tax penalties for withdrawal of your earnings before age 59½, and there may also be penalty charges imposed by annuity sponsors for withdrawals before a specified number of years have elapsed. Annuity sponsors may also charge annual maintenance fees, which reduce the annuity's effective yield. So read the fine print.

Hiring an Investment Manager

If you want a chicken dinner, you can buy some chicken at the supermarket and make your own dinner, or you can go to KFC and get a carryout and take it home, or go to a restaurant and have it served to you, maybe even on fancy china with linen napkins. In investing, too, you can decide what degree of involvement you want in choosing and managing your assets and also what degree of personalized service you want and need.

You can sit by yourself and make your own investment decisions. You can seek the help of a broker in selecting individual stocks and bonds in which to invest your money. Or you can ask your broker to help you choose a mutual fund or unit investment trust, which will then invest your money for you in an assortment of securities.

However, the ultimate in delegating the management of your finances is to hire your own investment manager and give him or her discretion over your assets. There are thousands and thousands of investment management firms available. If you have at least $100,000 to invest, you can hire one of those firms. For smaller accounts, your "individual" management will actually be pretty much "off-the-rack" management—i.e., the manager will do the same for your portfolio as he or she does for lots of other portfolios.

As the level of your assets increases, however, you can get truly custom-tailored investment management. Personalized management may ensure that you pursue the right investment goals, but it doesn't guarantee that you will achieve those goals any more than any other approach to investing.

Unless your portfolio gets up into the six-digit range, you are probably going to receive just as much attention working closely with your broker or choosing mutual funds whose investment objectives parallel yours. If you want to benefit from your broker's expertise, however, you need to concentrate your activities with a single broker. That way, you not only become a big enough client to generate attention, but more important, you also make it possible for the broker to develop a good overview of your financial picture.

Putting It All Together

The various vehicles for organizing and managing your investment are by no means mutually exclusive. When you're just starting out, mutual funds and unit investment trusts are a good way to get into the market because they provide immediate expertise and diversification. As your assets grow, and your investment knowledge increases, you can and should work closely with a broker in making direct investments in securities. As your wealth grows further, and your tax burden increases, you should be increasingly attuned to ways of deferring taxes. You should be putting money into a 401(k) plan from your first day on any job that offers such a plan. As your income and assets become more substantial, you should also explore other ways of deferring taxes, including IRAs and annuities.

If you prosper mightily and your portfolio gets to be substantial, you may wish to continue to work with your broker, or you may ask him or her to help you find an investment manager to provide portfolio management tailored to your precise needs. You'll get not only the investments you want but also a sensitivity to your needs and wishes with regard to estate planning and other highly individualized investment issues.

None of these alternatives rules out any of the others. A proper portfolio should probably include direct investments in various securities, plus mutual funds, plus investments in annuities and other tax-deferred investments, and if your assets get to be substantial, you can also put some of your money in the hands of a discretionary investment manager.

The Need to Diversify

By now you should have enough investment instruments and vehicles to hold you for a while. Can't decide which one to buy? Good. Because you shouldn't buy just one. Diversification is the best way to reduce risk in an unpredictable world. Interest rates may rise or fall. The stock market may shoot up, or plummet, or do nothing at all. Your income may double and you won't have to touch your investments for years. Or you may lose your job and have to cash in some investments to tide you over while you look for a new job.

You never know. That's why your portfolio has to be capable of benefiting from different investment environments and different scenarios in your personal life. Most investors will want portfolios that combine some current income with some chance for long-term growth, some liquidity and some of the high yields available in illiquid investments, some rock-solid securities and a couple of high fliers. You'll want to "ladder" your fixed-income investments so that they mature at different points in time. That way, you'll not only have cash becoming available if you need it without having to sell something prematurely, you will also gain protection against the continual changes in interest rates. It's true that by diversifying your investments, you'll always have put less money than you could have in those investments that turn out to be big winners, but you'll also have invested less than you might have in those that turn out to be losers. And you'll be ready for whatever twists and turns emerge, both in the markets and in your personal financial life. Taking a balanced approach will leave you far ahead of the game.

Look at the table on page 60 again. Remember, you don't want all your X's in a single row. That's great in bingo, but not in investing.

Now, on to the stock market. . . .

CHAPTER 6

THE STOCK MARKET

The Long-term View

It's a nice fantasy to imagine what your bank account would look like today if you had been around and buying stocks following the Great Crash of 1929. In the aftermath of that spectacular stock market collapse, which saw paper fortunes crumble into dust and investors head for the windows of tall buildings, the prices of common stocks sank to amazing lows. An investor with great foresight and a strong stomach could have picked up shares of General Motors for $9 apiece; 71 years later, each of those shares would be worth more than $1,000. Similarly, those who bought IBM for $68 a share in 1930 would have stock worth more than $200,000 in mid-2000.

But what if you had bought stock shortly before the Great Crash? What if you had bought into the market at precisely the wrong time, when stock prices had been driven to then-record highs in a roaring bull market by the doomed owners of pyramiding paper fortunes? Where would you stand today if you had bought stock at those inflated pre-Crash prices and held it ever since?

Just fine.

In the seven decades after 1926, the average share of common stock listed on the New York Stock Exchange appreciated (assuming you reinvested dividends) at a compound annual rate of about 10.6 percent, according to figures compiled by Ibbotson Associates, an investment consulting firm.

This 10.6 percent is an average that takes into account the stocks of companies that have gone out of business as well as those that have prospered mightily. It's important to note that this average falls only a little bit—to 9.9 percent—if the starting point for the portfolio is moved from 1926 to shortly before the Great Crash. The average is only slightly higher—about 10.0 percent—if figured for a portfolio purchased shortly after the Great Crash.

These figures, which also include the stock market crash of October 1987, compare with a compound annual inflation rate over the same years of about 3 percent, and a compound rate of return on corporate bonds of 5.6 percent, according to Ibbotson. In short, despite the ups and downs of the stock market, over the long term and on average, stocks have been an outstanding investment. There have been two reasons for this:

1. Stock prices tend, at the very least, to keep pace with inflation. That's because shares of stock represent shares of real things owned and produced by the issuing corporations, and an increase in the price of things is, after all, what is meant by inflation.

2. American corporations have done an excellent job of mobilizing people, technology, and natural resources to create wealth, and stock issued by those corporations appreciates to reflect that wealth creation. One common measure of corporate wealth creation is the statistic known as "return on equity." "Equity," in this case, refers to a corporation's net worth; "return" is profit. The average annual return on equity of American corporations over the last seventy years or so has been about 10 percent. It is no coincidence that on average

the stock of those corporations has appreciated at about the same rate.

The long-term advantages of stocks may seem dubious when the stock market hits the skids, but it is precisely at those times that it is most important to think in the long term. In October 1987, stock prices collapsed in a frightening rush, but after the crash of '87, guess what? At the bottom of this roller-coaster ride, stock prices were at about the level they had occupied a year earlier. A year earlier, investors had been thrilled to have their stocks reach that level. During the intervening months, as stocks roared up in one of the greatest bull markets in history, some investors made the mistake of thinking the good times would last indefinitely. But the market always turns. When it did, in a remarkably dramatic fashion, it took coolness and perspective to remember that the very prices then being bemoaned had been celebrated only a year before. People who had been investing steadily over a period of years (the bull market had begun in 1982) may have had their illusions shattered, but not their net worth. Most long-term investors still had substantial profits. The big losers were people who had been attempting to "play" the market during its great upward leap, jumping in and out for short-term gains. When the market crashed, they learned very painfully that playing the market is a dangerous game.

After the 1987 crash, the market embarked on a great rise in value. The Dow Jones Industrial Average, which was at 2695 in mid-1987 and fell to 1616 on October 20, 1987, had risen to 2634 at the end of 1990 and 5117 at the end of 1995. Then in mid-1996, the stock market fell out of bed once again. The Dow fell 345 points in just ten trading days. And then, guess what, it resumed its climb, and by autumn 1996 the Dow was over 6000. In early 1997, the Dow crossed the 7000 mark. But in the summer of 1998, the Dow fell sharply amid financial problems in Russia, Asia and Latin America. Moreover, there was also concern because of financial reversals suffered by a

The Dow Jones Industrial Average (1929-2000)

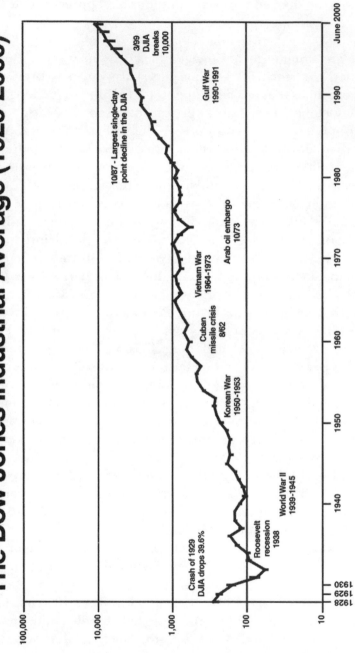

large hedge fund called Long Term Capital Management. In autumn, however, the Dow started back up and by the spring of 1999, it had climbed into the stratosphere, topping 10,000. At the beginning of 2000, it briefly surpassed 11,000 before settling back to the mid-10,000s.

The stock market's long-term track record for building wealth shows no signs of diminishing. Indeed, it may even be improving, as technological advances spur corporate productivity and, as a result, profitability. But I believe the increased market volatility of the past few years is here to stay, making it more important than ever for investors to focus on the long term. In the past, it was the role of the market makers or specialists in a given stock to cushion any sharp swings in the share price, ensuring an orderly market. Today, as ever-faster computer networks allow the almost instantaneous transfer of information around the world, the ability of intermediaries to modulate price fluctuations has diminished significantly. With the move to price all stocks in decimals, rather than fractions, bid-asked spreads are narrowing even further, and even more dramatic day-to-day price shifts may be in the offing. So, now more than ever, I caution against trying to "time" the market.

Don't "Play" the Market

There are two reasons why people lose money in the stock market. One has to do with the stocks they choose to buy, the other with when they choose to buy or sell them. Simply put, you can lose if you buy the wrong stock, or if you buy the right stock at the wrong time.

The fundamental reason why people lose money in the stock market is that they forget why they're there. You should enter the stock market for one reason only: to associate your capital with wealth-creating enterprises. This may sound too obvious to mention—why else does someone buy a share of stock?—but in fact, this goal is often forgotten by people who should know better. This is partly a result of the necessary abstractions of modern life. When you buy a share of General Motors, nobody comes to your house and hands you the unpainted door of a Buick or a drill used in assembling Oldsmobiles. That may be approximately what you have just purchased, but it would hardly be efficient to let every stockholder in a corporation take his or her piece of the company home every night. Instead, the assets of the corporation are recorded in the shorthand of numbers, and ownership shares of the corporation are represented by pieces of paper. (Increasingly, the paper is being supplanted by electronic entries on computerized ledgers.)

These "securities" are what change hands on the nation's stock exchanges, and people tend to talk about them as if they themselves were the things being invested in. But in fact, when you buy stock in a corporation you are buying a share of a vast collection of productive assets and a complex human organization, even if all that you see is a piece of paper.

Sometimes these pieces of paper are sold at a profit and sometimes they are sold at a loss. Often a security passes through dozens of hands without anyone involved ever laying eyes on the very real assets the paper represents. People who own the paper keep track of its price by looking at numbers on other pieces of paper, and there is often no clear and immediate connection between changes in that price and changes in the real world represented by the stock certificate. The price goes up, the price goes down. It begins to feel like an enormous game of chance—Las Vegas with stock-price-quotation machines. Everybody knows somebody who has made a fortune in high tech stocks yet doesn't know a silicon chip from a semiconductor. So why does it matter what's happening back at the factories and stores represented by the stock certificates? On Wall Street you can trade pieces of paper and make a lot of money doing it.

Not so fast. It's true that fortunes have been made trading those pieces of paper with hardly a thought given to what they represent. And it's very easy to get caught up in all this—

watching stock prices flash on CNBC all day and wondering "Which way is the market going?" You may get lucky for a while. If you have entered the market during one of its periodic great advances, you will do very well indeed buying a stock, holding it for a while, selling it at a profit, and then buying another and repeating the process. When the market begins one of its periodic declines, however, you will not do so well, unless you are one of the rare geniuses who can tell precisely when the switch in direction has arrived. But there's a saying on Wall Street: "They don't ring a bell at the top of the market."

In the long run, if you invest this way, you're going to lose. If you get caught up in the game of trading pieces of paper for a profit, you will find yourself making a lot of trades. You will constantly be trying to buy stocks that are about to go up in price, and sell stocks that are about to go down. Every time you make a trade, you will be buying from somebody, or selling to somebody. It's very easy to forget that there is another human being on the other side of every trade you make. Because of the way the market works, you almost never know who that other person is. But you should always remember that you are dealing with another person, and that person probably thinks you are wrong. He or she has decided to sell the stock you have decided to buy.

You think it's underpriced and about to move up. He thinks it's a turkey and it's time to bail out. One of you will turn out to be right, and one will turn out to be wrong. Short-term stock trading is a zero-sum game, where one side's gain is equal to the other's loss.

How often do you think you can win? By the law of averages, if the market moved randomly (and it doesn't), you should win half the time, just as you would if you were flipping coins. But if you do win half the time, you will still lose, because you may be paying brokerage commissions every time you trade, or incurring other kinds of fees. To come out ahead, you have to bat more than .500; you have to be right more often than the people on the other side of your trades.

But who are these people whom you must consistently out-smart? Are they a bunch of blithering idiots? ("Only a moron would sell that stock with the market moving the way it is!") In fact, they're probably reasonably intelligent people. In fact, many of them are probably just as smart as you. And some of them are undoubtedly smarter. Some of them are million-aires who have made their fortunes in the stock market over many years of trading. Some of them are the managers of vast mutual funds, who have batteries of computers and battalions of well-trained analysts guiding their every move. Some of them may even be executives of the very corporations whose stock you are buying and selling, executives who know a lot more than you do about what's happening at the company.

And who are you?

Well, you may say, I'm no dummy. And besides, I've got some expert advice in my corner too. I have this broker who really seems to know what she's doing. Last month alone, she made me $1,200.

That's nice, but if she's so smart how come she's not rich? Why isn't she cabling in her own market orders from her yacht off Bimini? How come she has to work for you?

Neither she nor anyone else knows which way the market is going over the short term. Anyone who says they have figured it out is deluded, or mistaken, or dishonest. Trying to win the short-term game in the stock market can be tremendously exciting. But you had better decide right now whether you want to get rich or you want to have fun. If you enjoy match-ing your wits against others and absorbing yourself in com-plex intellectual games, I recommend that you take up bridge or chess. They're not quite as much fun as the stock market, but they're a whole lot cheaper.

The path you should take in stock market investing is a slow and often boring one. It requires patience and discipline and a lot of waiting. It's not nearly as much fun as attempting to trade pieces of paper at a profit, but it does offer one nice consolation: It can help you achieve your goal of financial serenity.

Picking Stocks

Long-term investing in stocks is a positive-sum game (one in which all the players can come out ahead), because over the long term, most American corporations create real wealth and the prices of their shares rise to reflect that wealth creation. Nevertheless, there are also some real stinkers out there. There are stocks that go down and then down some more; there are companies that go belly-up. The 10 percent average annual appreciation of American stocks over the last seven decades has been calculated by combining the records of companies that have prospered immensely, single-handedly making their shareholders wealthy, with those of companies that have tortured their shareholders with endlessly declining fortunes.

Which stocks are you going to buy?

The first step (but only the first step) in making that decision is identifying a good company. The bad ones don't wear little signs saying "I'm a Stinker," but the good ones do possess certain identifiable characteristics. Mr. Dean Witter summed them up in a 1963 speech: "I shall again repeat the hackneyed advice to recommend stocks of good, well-known, and well-established companies with a long history of successful operation."

Picking such companies is really just a matter of common sense. You want a company that has honest, effective managers and is producing a product or service that people want and need. The company should be offering that product or service to the market at an attractive price, and it should have demonstrated its mastery of the many steps in the chain between the creation of a product and its delivery to the consumer. The company should be comfortable with complexity and uncertainty, and it should be able to adapt to change, because there will be significant changes in its field, whatever its field may be. The company should have an enlightened attitude toward its own employees, and it should have its financial house in order.

You may know of such companies through your own direct experience. Perhaps you work for one, or buy the products of one. You may read about such companies in your local newspaper or in the financial press. Your broker will certainly have some candidates to recommend, backed by detailed analyses prepared by the research department of the brokerage firm.

You may want to investigate your candidate companies further by inspecting their annual reports. Of course, according to most annual reports, every company is a great company; just look at the glowing reports from management nestled between the glossy photographs of smiling employees. There are a few honest exceptions. Years ago, an Oregon high-technology company called Tektronix amazed annual-reports aficionados by acknowledging, "That dill-pickle look on your face says you have just read our Highlights, as they are euphemistically called. . . . Our earnings took a pasting." But such candor is rare.

To get the most out of annual reports, you should read them from back to front. In the back, amid the financial tables and the fine-print footnotes, is generally where you'll find the most important indicators of a company's health. Among the things to look for here is the ratio of the company's assets to its debt; a healthy ratio is generally at least two to one. This figure may be distorted, however, by the inclusion of some dubious assets. If a significant share of assets are listed under the heading "intangibles," for example, check the footnotes to see what those intangibles are. A company may put a higher price tag on its "goodwill" than anyone else would.

Another component of a company's assets is its inventory of unsold goods. If the inventory is only a small fraction of the company's annual sales, that means its products are selling at a respectable pace and are almost certainly worth what the company says they are. If the inventory is building up, on the other hand, it may be that nobody wants to buy their slide rules anymore. The inventory's value may be overstated because the only way to sell the products being stored may be to sharply reduce prices.

One of the most widely cited figures in a company's financial statement is its earnings per share of stock outstanding. It's heartwarming to see earnings per share go up at a steady rate over a number of years. But when you look at this number, take note of whether increased earnings come from ongoing sales of products, or if they come from some extraordinary one-shot transaction that may have been made just to pump up earnings. An attractive company usually should be selling a larger amount of its products every year. It can only sell its headquarters building once.

There are a whole set of well-established techniques for looking at a company's financial reports and assessing its health. You don't need to spend two years in graduate school earning an M.B.A. degree to learn at least some of these techniques. And when you apply them, they won't tell you everything. Financial analysis is like a doctor checking every patient's blood pressure and other vital signs: it's a quick way of zeroing in on who looks pretty healthy and who doesn't.

Sometimes, of course, all this careful analysis seems beside the point—some stocks seem to defy the laws of gravity and rise without any regard to their underlying results. Such was the case with many stocks that had anything to do with the Internet. The enthusiasm for the "dot.com" stocks that began to unfold in the late 1990s was the successor to a series of fixations with this or that industry. Eventually, and inevitably, these industries begin to be treated like other industries, and traditional analytic techniques are accepted by most investors. Until then, you need to exercise special caution before investing in these areas.

What Is a Stock Worth?

Assuming you have done your homework and have identified some successful, healthy, honest corporations, should you rush right out and buy their stocks? Not necessarily. You may be the ten millionth person this week to identify that company as a winner. Nine million of those people may already be in the market trying to buy the stock, waving hundred-dollar bills around and bidding up its price.

The stock of a good company is not necessarily a good buy at any price. In fact, it's only a good buy if it's available at a price equal to, or less than, its proportionate share of the company's value. Granted, value is a somewhat subjective term, but at least it is grounded in reality. What dividend is the company paying? What is its net worth (its assets minus its debts)? What are its prospects for the future? All of these are components of value.

Price, unlike value, is completely subjective. It is whatever somebody is willing to pay for something at a given moment. It is subject to individual whims and to the many kinds of mass psychology that move the stock market through its cycles. Wall Street continuously abounds with significant disparities between price and value. These disparities will give you the chance to make some excellent investments, if you're capable of independent thinking. Such thinking will be required because disparities between price and value are always accompanied by rationalizations "explaining" the discrepancy. The greater the discrepancy, the more widely believed the rationalization is, and thus the more intimidating it is to question it.

All right then, what is a stock worth? This is the conventional way to phrase the question, but I believe it obscures the main point. The better question is this: What is the company worth compared to what it is selling for? It's relatively simple to calculate this, so I'm flabbergasted at how few people, including investment professionals, ever get around to making the calculation.

You can easily calculate a company's "market capitalization." It is the price of a share times the number of shares outstanding. A company with 10 million shares of stock outstanding, each one selling for $1, has a market capitalization of $10 million. A company with 1 million shares outstanding, each one selling for $10, has the same market capitalization. Thus, investors have placed the same value on the company, even though a share of its stock is selling for ten times as much. The differences in statistics figured on a per-share basis without taking into consideration the number of shares outstanding will sometimes obscure significant differences in value.

One way of comparing the prices investors assign to comparable values is to look at the price/earnings ratio (P/E) of various stocks. The P/E is the price per share divided by a company's annual earnings per share. If a stock is selling for $50 and the company is earning $6 per share, the stock's P/E is 8.3.

If all companies were equally promising, all stocks would sell at the same P/E ratio. Earnings per share, after all, are a fairly objective measurement of the return one can expect from a stock. Some of those earnings are paid out in dividends. Some of them are reinvested in the company, increasing the value of its assets and its potential for future earnings.

Companies whose prospects are highly regarded by investors, however, sell for higher P/E ratios than other companies. To associate your capital with highly regarded enterprises, you must accept less favorable terms in order to persuade the current holders of the securities to give up their shares in what promise to be successful ventures. Shortly after the stock of Apple Computer went on sale in the 1980s, the public was so enamored of its potential that it sold at a P/E of 150. In 1985, the stock of a company called Cardio Pet, which performed electrocardiograms on dogs, was selling at a P/E of 200. As in the case of Apple, investors were extremely bullish on the company's future. In the mid-1990s, with the Internet all the rage, Netscape Communications, a company whose software helped people surf the Net, went public, and its shares were soon selling for 355 times its earnings at a time when the market as a whole was selling for about 16 times earnings. And by the end of the decade, "dot.com" start-ups with no prospect of generating positive earnings for years were commanding hundreds of dollars per share, while many profitable "old economy" stocks were selling at price/earning multiples of less than ten.

Occasionally, such investor confidence is justified, but more often it is not. Apple was and is a fine company, but at a P/E of 150, the price of its stock was definitely inflated. (It later fell precipitously.)

Cardio Pet—another high-tech shooting star—suffered a worse fate, filing for bankruptcy by mid-1985. As for many Internet high-flyers, the jury is still out. A sharp sell-off in early 2000 brought valuations down considerably—by more than half, on average. And investors have begun to be more discriminating among the "dot.coms," sticking with the market leaders and taking a more critical look at the myriad of new ventures that have gone public in recent years.

Nevertheless, many investors are prone to climb on one bandwagon or other and to pay unreasonable prices for whatever stocks are the darlings of the moment. These fads usually have their origin in some genuinely shrewd observation about the worth of a particular type of security. That observation (e.g., "The Internet changes everything") is gradually coming to be understood by more and more people; they act on it by buying the stocks in question, and this rewards those who first saw and acted on the insight. Eventually, everybody and his uncle is chasing after the stocks, bidding them up past their original, underpriced state and carelessly applying the original observation to all similar-looking stocks without discrimination. Ultimately people figure out that the Emperor is naked, and the boom collapses.

These bandwagons do create solid investment opportunities in a way. As they go tearing through the market, the stocks they leave behind may be very good bargains indeed. In 1984, for example, a number of oil company stocks could have been purchased at a price per share that was actually less than the per-share market value of their proven oil and gas reserves (minus long-term debt). The diligent investigator can almost always find a selection of stocks selling at low P/E ratios, and even some selling for less than "book value" (the per-share value of the company's net worth).

Of course, such statistically cheap stocks may be cheap for a good reason (and therefore may not really be cheap at all). Apparent bargains must be carefully investigated. Do their low prices reflect major problems? Or have they been unfairly underpriced by a trendy market that is chasing a trend somewhere else? The drawback here is that a trend, however misguided you may think it is, can continue for a long time. Consequently, when you buy the underpriced stock of an unjustly overlooked company, you must be prepared to sit and hold your stock until other investors come to their senses and recognize its value.

In the late 1970s, one place to look for underpriced stocks was among the low-priced shares of small companies. The huge pension funds and other institutional investors that were assuming a major role in the market devoted most of their attention to the "nifty fifty" (fifty or so well-established, high profile companies) and tended to ignore the rest. The rest of the market tended to outperform the nifty fifty, however, and eventually the institutional investors caught on. They shifted their attention to the "nifty fifth," the stocks in the bottom fifth (pricewise) of those listed on the New York Stock Exchange.

What happened then was that the inflow of all this institutional money created price distortions in the market. Suddenly, the shares of obscure small companies were selling for relatively higher prices than those of major corporations, for no fundamentally sound reason. Shrewd investors kept an eye on the situation and watched for bargains. Occasionally a crowd of big buyers would rush into a small company's stock on the basis of glowing predictions of future earnings. The price would soar. Then an actual earnings report would be issued that fell short of the predictions. It would not necessarily be bad news, just disappointing news compared to what had been expected. Major holders would sell the stock in droves. The price would dive. What had been overpriced days before was now underpriced. Observant investors moved in and picked up a bargain. That kind of thing happens all the time in the stock market. Big institutions have access to reams of research and analysis from their own staff as well as from securities firms. Yet they're also driven by the same kind of herd instincts that prompt small investors to do what they see everybody else doing. Consequently, if you have the independence to zig when others are zagging, you can often end up getting bargains and profiting handsomely.

The Blue-chip Option

Finding underpriced stocks is, of course, easier said than done. It's one thing to master some principles of analysis; it's another to leap into the universe of ten thousand or so stocks and start sorting through financial data and making decisions.

Your broker should be able to help you here. Backed by his or her research department's reports, your broker can give you all the help you need to select stocks that are truly good values.

But the final decision to buy will still be up to you. You may enjoy making these decisions, or the process may give you a permanent stomachache. If you are in the latter camp, you have a couple of other good options.

One of these is to concentrate your investments in "blue-chip" stocks. These are the most visible stocks on Wall Street, issued by well-known large corporations with long records of success—General Electric, Ford Motor Company, Exxon-Mobil, Coca-Cola, Du Pont . . . you get the idea. In the past, certain people confined their investments to these companies simply because blue-chip stocks seemed to represent the stuff of wisdom, forbearance, morality, and, above all, good breeding. No rude little upstart companies for these investors. They bought their 10,000 shares of General Electric and then departed on their six-month world cruise with no intention of interrupting their relaxation for anything so vulgar as checking a stock price.

But there is some method to this madness. Blue-chip companies are so large, so well established, so enmeshed in the American economy that they are almost certain to continue to prosper as long as the country does. They may falter for a while, as they did at the turn of the century—2000, not 1900—but it is unlikely that they will fall. It is more likely that they will solve whatever problems they face and continue to dominate their industries. Consumers are accustomed to buying the brands they produce. Their reputations attract a steady stream of young talent. Their top executives are well tested in the marketplace. Because of their sheer size, these companies attract substantial amounts of journalistic and governmental scrutiny; they can't help but deal with their problems. Moreover, investor attention may drift to whatever is hot at the moment, but as that fad inevitably cools, many investors come back to the tried and true.

Investing in blue-chip stocks is certainly no way to get rich quick. Unlike new, small, hungry companies, the blue-chip giants are too big, and generally too conservative, to make daring moves that might double or triple the price of their stock in a year. But the flip side of this is that the same size and market position limiting the possibility of spectacular growth also helps ensure continuing moderate growth. Companies that have big, well-established businesses generally don't fall apart overnight. If you can find companies that achieve steady moderate growth year after year—say, at the average historical rate of 10 percent—that's enough to make you wealthy over the course of your long-term investment program.

If this sounds just too boring, there is one wrinkle in the

blue-chip strategy you might want to try. Concentrate on the thirty stocks in the Dow Jones Industrial Average, and keep track of their yields. These indicate which of the stocks are currently most favored by investors and which are least favored. History has demonstrated that the Dow Jones thirty periodically rotate through this in-favor, out-of-favor cycle; this year's darling was last year's dog. So it might make sense to buy the highest-yielding stocks on the list, hold them for a year, then sell them and buy whichever Dow stocks have replaced them at the top of the list. There is no guarantee that every high-yielding stock in the group will rise, of course, but the past is on your side here, and it is, at least, unlikely that the company will go belly-up while you are waiting for history to repeat itself.

Mutual Funds

One increasingly popular way to invest in the stock market while avoiding the agonies of decision making is to buy shares in a mutual fund that invests in stocks. As noted in the previous chapter, mutual funds offer several advantages, including diversification and professional management.

Because of the growth of interest in mutual funds, their numbers increased sharply in the 1990s, and the range of strategies and specialties offered by mutual funds has expanded as well. There are thousands of funds investing only in stocks, and they have a wide assortment of different techniques. Some funds seek out stocks that pay high dividends. Others seek stocks with the potential for long-term growth. Still others aim for a combination of income and growth. Some funds specialize in the stocks of small, high-risk companies. Others seek stocks that are fundamentally good values but seem to be underpriced in the current market. There are funds that specialize in the stocks of gold-mining companies, high-tech companies, foreign companies, or companies from the emerging markets—the rapidly growing nations in Asia and Latin America. The list goes on and on.

Each fund's philosophy is spelled out in a prospectus. You should read prospectuses carefully and pick a fund that shares your investment philosophy and goals—and your level of tolerance for risk.

The distinct differences in the approaches and philosophies that guide fund managers in their selection of stocks produce sharp differences in their investment results.

For example, during the twelve months ending June 30, 1998, the Standard & Poor's 500 Stock Index rose 22.76 percent. During the same one-year period, according to Lipper, Inc., mutual funds specializing in the stocks of smaller companies rose 1.84 percent, while those focusing on science and technology stocks rose 66.28 percent, international funds rose 4.84 percent, and growth and income funds rose 14.5 percent. And, of course, each of those categories contains dozens, sometimes hundreds of funds, and there were also wide disparities in the returns they achieved. More recently, there has been a wide divergence between the returns achieved by mutual funds focused on high-tech stocks and those investing in other sectors of the economy.

You should certainly check the past performance of any fund in which you're considering investing. But keep in mind that past performance is no guarantee of future results. Many funds do well for several years and then, as market trends or the economy turn against the kind of stock they specialize in, they take a downward turn and spend several years in the cellar. Or the investment manager who has guided the fund to its success leaves for another job and his or her successor turns out not to have the same good judgment and the fund falters.

In addition to investment philosophy and performance, another attribute you need to think about is whether a fund you're considering investing in is part of a "family" of mutual funds with different investment philosophies. Often you are allowed to switch your money freely from fund to fund within the family at no charge, so you can move your investments in response to changes in market conditions, changes in your views about which investment philosophy is about to be rewarded, or in response to changes in your financial situation. This flexibility makes it a little easier for you to manage your assets.

Hope, Boredom, Greed, and Fear

Whether you select individual stocks or a mutual fund, you should be buying securities that you intend to own for a long time. Remember, you are investing, not trading pieces of paper in search of a quick profit. You are looking not for stocks that will double in price in five days but for stocks that will double in price in five years. You are seeking out companies that are well positioned to create wealth well into the future, and you should be prepared to stick with them as they do so.

This is the kind of resolution that is easier to honor in theory than in practice. Working against your resolve to buy worthy stocks and to hold them will be some very formidable enemies: hope, boredom, greed, and fear. They have undone the best of us.

Hope will encourage you to hold on to a stock when you have made a serious mistake. (Your general rule should be to hold stocks for a long time, but this rule should not be carved in stone. Sometimes major changes in the market or the economy mean you should abandon a position. More about this in Chapter 11.) Hope will entice you into adopting the Lighter-Than-Air Syndrome—i.e., the belief that what goes down must come back up. It ain't necessarily so. You must be ruthlessly objective and try to determine whether you are hanging on to a loser because the company is fundamentally sound, or because of the siren song of hope.

Boredom will entice you into selling stocks that you know are fundamentally sound but are just so . . . dull. Even a stock that is going from $10 to $100 in five years is certain to spend many days, weeks, or months doing nothing much at all. Its upward moves will tend to come in exhilarating spurts; the long periods in between may bore you to death. It is very tempting to sell a successful but dull investment to get aboard something more exciting. Your desire to do so will, of course, be accompanied by elaborate rationalizations explaining why your successful but boring stock has really reached its peak and why its more exciting competitor is really a fabulous buy.

Greed and fear, the most powerful emotions you will encounter, are children of the great "bull" and "bear" markets that periodically sweep through Wall Street in cycles that are, to say the least, imperfectly understood. A bull market occurs when stocks go up and up and up. Everybody is making money. Everybody is happy. A bear market, conversely, is when stocks go down and down, and everybody is unhappy except the "bears," who have "sold short" or otherwise arranged their affairs to profit from a declining market. (More about these strategies in Chapter 10.)

When a bull market first begins, it is generally not recognized. When, eventually, it is recognized, its cause is rarely clear. As it builds, people find reasons to explain it. The longer the bull market lasts, the clearer those explanations become, until, finally, everybody "knows" why the boom began and, moreover, why it is certain to continue for a good long time. This moment of clarity usually occurs immediately before the bull market collapses.

Participating in a bull market is something like eating a pizza. You wait a long time for it to arrive. When it first comes it is too hot to touch. Then you get in some good bites, but before you are finished, it cools down and loses its appeal.

During the tastiest part of a bull market, stock prices soar to dizzying heights, carried along by their own momentum. People who wouldn't have paid $10 a share for a stock three months before will stand in line to buy it for $20. Has the fundamental value of the company changed? Almost certainly not. Only the market has changed. And people are getting greedy. They are buying stocks because stocks are going up.

What they buy today for $20 they will sell next week for $22. And why not? The price went up $2 last week, didn't it?

Even those wise enough to see that the Emperor has no clothes may go along for the ride. They are operating on the "Greater Fool Theory." They know darn well that National Slide Rule is ludicrously overpriced at $20 a share, but they expect they can sell it to some greater fool at an even more ludicrous price in a few days.

Your overriding objective in a roaring bull market is to avoid becoming the Greatest Fool at the end of the line. When everything you touch is turning to gold, when you are confident that stock prices will continue to soar, when your barber starts to tell you about his latest triumphs in the market, whisper these words to yourself: "I really don't know what I'm doing. I am not a genius." And get out.

Inevitably, the market will turn. Success will turn to dullness, then dullness will turn to disappointment. You may take to having a martini as you watch the evening news and review the diminution of your wealth. As the bear market gains momentum, additional drinks may become useful in putting the whole unpleasant business out of mind. The market keeps tumbling. You've lost all your paper profits. The market tumbles further. Will you lose everything? Out of moments like these come decisions to sell stocks at rock-bottom prices.

These panicky sellouts are major mistakes. If you have selected a stock with care, then you should not be concerned if its price is down. You bought it to hold it, so hold it. What you should be doing, in fact, during a plummeting market is not selling but buying. Value often increases as prices decline. If you bought a stock at $20, and it was a good buy at that price, then it is a much better buy at $10. The legendary investor Bernard Baruch made a point of stepping up his purchases of stocks he liked when their prices went down, and the practice contributed to his fortune. Mr. Dean Witter, during the depths of the Depression, advised clients, "Buy now. The present offers splendid opportunities." You too can pick up excellent bargains by taking advantage of the despair of demoralized investors—if you can only avoid the all-too-human tendency to panic along with everybody else and become one of the demoralized investors yourself.

If you can keep your head when those around you are losing theirs, you can prosper in the stock market. The stock market is one race that is often won not by the swift but rather by those who are slow and steady. Ultimately, that insight may be worth more than a pile of hot tips on the market.

CHAPTER 7

THE ELECTRONIC REVOLUTION MEETS WALL STREET

Technology, the Internet, and Your Investments

Once not much more than an improvement on the typewriter and calculator, the computer—especially in the age of the Internet—now touches almost every aspect of our lives. You can send e-mails, read the newspaper, check the current weather in Switzerland, and even buy a car with a few clicks of your mouse. And investing and other areas of personal finance are no exception to the electronic revolution. Today, you can do investment research, trading and record keeping all with your personal computer.

On-line investing has been legitimized in the past few years. Not so long ago, on-line investing was the territory of day traders, chat room rumor mills, and get-rich-quick schemes. But today, many investors focused on long-term financial goals are using the Internet as a financial tool. In response, many of the major brokerage firms now offer their clients the ability to make transactions on-line. They also provide a vast number of educational tools, research, and opportunities for obtaining advice through the Web.

On-line investing can be a boon for investors who prefer to do their own investment research and want to take charge of their finances in a hands-on sort of way. However, if you're going to invest on-line, arm yourself with knowledge and proceed with caution.

Investors who may not have a tight grasp on their financial situation and goals, or who don't have the discipline to invest for the long-term, risk falling prey to overactive trading. Or, they invest based on rumors and tips from unreliable sources—and as a result are likely to lose big. Understanding your own personal financial goals and following the same long-term approach we've discussed throughout this book is something you'll never get from the Web. But it's the key to successful on-line investing.

Let's examine how technology and the Internet have changed investing by looking at three phases of the investment process: analysis and selection of investments, conducting transactions, and portfolio management.

Analysis and Selection

Traditionally, the process of analyzing potential investments starts with listening to the views of your broker. Or, you may talk to knowledgeable and trusted friends and advisors. You may also listen to ideas from market commentators on financial news programs and read articles in newspapers and magazines. Then, you follow up on ideas that seem promising by asking your broker for more information or contacting a company and asking for an annual report.

But today, the Web has shifted this whole process into hyperspeed, accelerating the pace at which information can be located and acquired. You can now receive all sorts of investment information—including a great deal of brokerage house research as well as Securities and Exchange Commission filings—on-line. And instead of making telephone calls or writing letters asking companies to mail you information, you can often download their annual reports and other information directly from their Web sites.

A vast assortment of analytics are also available. Are you the type of investor who's interested in examining ratios and patterns? Chances are someone has calculated or plotted whatever you want, and you can just download it.

In short, all of the information gathering and calculating that might have stretched over a couple of weeks can now be done very quickly at your computer.

It's true: There's a lot of valuable information available on-line. But, there's also a lot of bad information. A notable example is the information spread through investment chat rooms. At various appointed hours, people all over the world are busily typing in their news and views on stocks and markets in these electronic gathering places.

The trouble is, there are no admission requirements for chat rooms, nor any background checks or IQ tests. Many, like you, are presumably there to learn. But others may have axes to grind. Some want to promote a stock they own so they can boost its price, while others may talk down a stock to hurt a company or one of its investors. Why not help that price fall by spreading rumors to the effect that the company's products don't work or that it's about to lose a big contract? Especially with the stocks of smaller companies, these rumors can send prices on a roller coaster ride.

But even if chat room investors mean well, just keep asking yourself one question: "If this person knows so much, why is he or she in a chat room telling me?" If you decide to drop in on some investment chat rooms, take what you read with a grain of salt.

Chat rooms are just one example of what to avoid while researching investments. Successful investment research on the Web requires that you know that your source is credible. When viewing financial Web sites, make sure you know the reputation of your source and check out the credentials of their analysts. And remember, just because a Web site is well designed doesn't mean it has the best information.

Conducting Transactions

Until the mid-1990s, most investors bought or sold securities by making a decision in consultation with a broker and then instructing the broker to execute the transaction. After that, the broker would send an order to the floor of the New York Stock Exchange or to some other marketplace to either buy or sell something "at the market"—i.e., at prevailing prices—or as a "limit order"—i.e., to be executed only if it could be done at a specified price or better. All this took place during daylight hours.

But on-line investing has made it possible to send electronic instructions to a brokerage firm to buy or sell something without a broker. If you find an investment you like, you can purchase it at any time—often regardless of whether the market's open.

If you've done your research and are certain that the investment fits in with your investment objectives, it can be pretty convenient and for the most part relatively secure. However, even the most savvy investors can benefit from advice. The more often you trade independently, the more you may miss the advantage of discussing your decisions with a broker who may have news that would affect that decision. After all, your broker spends all day, every day, gathering investment information: His or her livelihood depends on it. With on-line trading, it becomes so easy to make a transaction that you may lose sight of the need to make decisions based on your long-term financial plan. Or, you may become an overactive trader. . .

Overactive Trading

On-line trading has created a whole new category of investor—the computer-based day trader. Actually, there have always been day traders—people who move in and out of investments many times over the course of the day. They used to watch the ticker tape in brokerage offices and were, in many cases, big-time professional investors. But with on-line investing, regular investors can morph into day traders, watching the market and entering trades via computer at home.

Day traders respond to movements in the market. The idea of day-trading is to eke out profits by say, buying XYZ Corp. at 10 A.M., selling it at 10:15 when it has gone up a few cents, buying it again at 10:45 because the price has dropped a bit, selling it at 11:05, and buying and selling it again several more times over the course of the day. People who fall into this category may know next to nothing about the companies they invest in. They just watch the gyrations of a company's stock price and plunge in and out, based on a belief that there are patterns in stock prices or through essentially random guesses at what will happen next.

While I trust you won't go so far as to quit your job and sit around all day in your pajamas trading stocks on-line, buying and selling frequently may be tempting (and is certainly easy to do) with on-line investing—but it's a temptation you must resist. Remember, what day traders are doing is speculating. And speculating is not only highly risky, it's more like gambling than true investing. In fact, the head of the North American Securities Administrators Association called day trading his organization's number-one concern and offered this advice to day traders: "Go to Las Vegas—the food is better."

Successful investing requires that you take a long-term, disciplined approach toward your financial goals. You should plan to hold on to the investments you purchase on-line just as if you were purchasing them through a broker.

Misusing After-hours Trading

Another symptom of overactive trading involves excessive use of extended-hours trading or after-hours trading. For years, the only times you could place a trade were during the hours the markets were open, which, since the early 1980s, has been 9:30 A.M. to 4:00 P.M. for the New York Stock Exchange. But with on-line investing, you can place trades 24 hours a day. You can tuck the children into bed, do the dishes, and then log on and electronically enter orders to buy and sell stocks.

With many on-line services that offer after-hours trading, you can place an order to be completed on the next business day during conventional market hours. If the only time you have to research and focus on investing is at night after work and household chores are complete, this can be a real convenience.

However, with extended-hours trading, you can place limit orders that can actually be executed after-hours, quite often within minutes after they've been placed. These transactions are completed through electronic communications networks (ECNs), which are computer networks that match buy and sell orders that are submitted electronically and consummate transactions without any human intervention. With this type of trading you need to be careful.

If you place an order after hours for execution the next day, you may not encounter any surprises. But if you want the transaction to be completed that night, you may find that the extended-hours price on your transaction is much different from what you'd find during the day. Why? In these relatively early days of extended-hours trading, there are not a whole lot of customers—and that can affect the price of an investment. Professor Jeremy Siegel of the University of Pennsylvania's Wharton School took a look at the earliest days of extended-hours trading and wrote, "During the evening and nighttime, a small trading volume will usually move the market far more than it would during the day. Bid-asked spreads will often be higher in off-hours, and it will be easier for professionals to 'run' a stock up or down and trigger stop orders left by other traders." In short, extended-hours investors may find themselves swept up in waves and currents they didn't expect, including some being generated by savvy professionals.

If you're looking for more certainty about the price you want to pay for an investment, enter the order to be executed for the next day when the markets are open and more people are trading. If you reach a decision at 8:00 at night that a certain stock is a good buy, you should be able to wait until the next morning to buy it. But if you *need* to buy it at 8:05 that night, there's a more fundamental issue: You may be more of a speculator than an investor. Remember, you should be expecting to hold on to the stock you purchase for months or years. Ditto if you want to sell. A decision to sell, like the decision to buy, should stand the test of time.

Now maybe you have learned some important news about the company, and you need to get in or out of the stock before the news impacts the price. But if you have acquired this information by watching CNN at 9 P.M., do you think you can rush to your computer and buy or sell the stock before the rest of the market? Are you the only person watching CNN? And with the hordes of securities analysts and portfolio managers who had an inkling that this news was coming, the price of the stock probably already reflects the news you just heard.

Portfolio Management

In my view, one of the ways your PC can be most useful is in managing your portfolio and keeping records. Programs like Quicken and Microsoft Money can be integrated with reports on your accounts at securities firms and banks to provide you with real-time summaries of your financial condition. Or, your brokerage firm may even offer account aggregation technology that can enable you to view all of your on-line accounts in one secure location. These programs also let you store some fairly arcane figures, like the original cost of various investments—a figure that can be important in determining the taxes on the investment that you sell. This helps you know where you started and where you are, and that's important in determining whether you're getting to where you want to go.

Pouring your financial life into your computer also helps break down the barriers of pocket accounting. When all your assets and liabilities are on the same screen, you're less likely to compartmentalize your investments. That helps you understand whether your portfolio is truly diversified or excessively concentrated in a limited range of investments. Not only that, but in your financial planning, you can experiment with different scenarios and models, and answer an assortment of "What if?" questions.

In short, technology and the Internet have provided a vast amount of new opportunities for individual investors. But never forget that technology is a tool—not a substitute for good judgment and rational decision-making. If you decide to invest on the Web, have your financial goals and game plan set before you invest. Know your limitations and tolerance for risk. Understand the investment choices you're about to make before you make them. And know where the information you find is coming from.

CHAPTER 8

REAL ESTATE

Is Real Estate for You?

Along with stocks, real estate is the most visible, feasible, and attractive kind of "owning" investment available to most Americans. Buying a house (or some other type of home) is the only real estate transaction many people will ever undertake. But millions of Americans have prospered mightily over the last few decades by selling their homes for much more than they paid for them. And millions of Americans have also done well by investing in real estate in addition to their own home.

Homeownership and real estate investing may very well make sense for you, but before you fall in love with that shabby but charming Victorian at the edge of downtown or decide you're going to make a quick million dollars with your own mini real estate empire, there are a few facts you ought to consider. Above all, you must remember there's nothing magical about real estate. If Santa Claus does not live on Wall Street, neither does he live in that potential turnaround neighborhood under the elevated expressway. You need to compare the potential return from a real estate investment to the returns available to you elsewhere.

Historically, real estate prices have moved up more or less in tandem with inflation, and property has generally been regarded as a good hedge against the effects of inflation. Real estate investors have often earned a return significantly better than the inflation rate by enhancing their properties through expansion or renovation. Real estate investors have also earned handsome returns by taking advantage of tax breaks and leverage. If the real estate you purchase is your own home, your return will be augmented as well by the opportunity to live in your investment. You can't live in a corporate bond. Nor can a stock provide a good view of the sunset. But over the years, a home can produce all sorts of psychic benefits—and generate a nice return as well.

Don't forget that money can easily be lost in real estate. When you own a piece of land or other property that you don't develop with additional investment dollars, you're not participating in the wealth-creation process, as you would be if you had purchased shares of stock. Your property is just sitting there. Whether or not it will increase in value depends largely on circumstances beyond your control. Neighborhoods boom and neighborhoods decay. While you're waiting to see which will happen to the neighborhood in question, your property will be costing you money—money for maintenance, taxes, and interest on the money you borrowed to buy the property—and you will also be missing out on the dividend or interest income you could have had if you had invested in something else.

If the value of your property quadruples in twenty years, that may sound terrific. But any other investment would quadruple in value in twenty years if it earned 7.2 percent annually. When you hear people talking about how the price of their home doubled or tripled, you have to think about the period of time involved. On the other hand (and there are some spectacular other hands in real estate), your humble little property could just be in the path of the future development of the next Disney World, in which case someone will pay you a bundle for it.

Over the long term, real estate investments have yielded returns roughly comparable to the average returns on common stocks. That shouldn't be surprising, because if it were otherwise, investors would have flocked to the market offering the best returns, and that would have driven returns in that market down to the level of the other market. Real estate, like stocks, has had periods of doing rather well and periods of sluggish returns. Nonetheless, on average and over the long term, equity or owning investments, like stocks and real estate, have generally done better than debt or lending investments.

For most investors, real estate and the stock market may well be the best places to put substantial portions of their long-term capital. The question is how to allocate your assets between these two equity investments. That, of course, is just part of the larger asset allocation question: How should you split up your money among all the various kinds of investments that seem suited to your needs?

Any discussion of real estate investing requires dividing the subject into two categories: buying a home and investing in real estate you're not going to live in, much less fall in love with. Buying a house is an investment in many ways, and in many ways it isn't. You don't have to own bonds, but you do have to live somewhere. And you'd probably like to live someplace nice. You need to think about the costs and rates of return associated with owning a house, but you also need to think about school districts and views.

The Appeal of Homeownership

Would you like to own your own home? Or would you prefer to rent for the rest of your life? If you're a normal, red-blooded American, your answer will be loud and clear. Homeownership is part of the American dream, the part where the kids are playing outside in the yard with the white picket fence, while you're relaxing in your own living room without hearing a neighbor's stereo blaring. Out back, near the swing set, there's a little garden where any year now you're going to get around to putting in some roses. It's not surprising that the United States has a higher percentage of owner-occupied homes than any other country in the world. Some two thirds of Americans own their own homes.

Home ownership is something most Americans aspire to, for a number of financial reasons. Rent payments disappear forever into your landlord's pockets and don't build up equity (ownership) in the property you inhabit, as payments on a home mortgage do. If you have taxable income and you qualify to itemize your tax deductions on Schedule A of your federal income tax, home ownership provides one of the last, great legal tax shelters offered by the federal government: the mortgage interest tax and local property tax deductions. That means the portion of your mortgage payment that goes to pay interest—and in the early years of a typical mortgage that's most of your monthly payment—can be deducted on your tax return. Moreover, a tax law change in 1997 made home ownership more attractive by making the gain on the sale of a personal residence tax free. For married couples, up to $500,000 in capital gains associated with the sale of a home is exempt from tax on a qualifying sale, and the figure is $250,000 for a single individual. This has made the benefits of homeownership even more attractive.

The second reason that home ownership is desirable to many Americans involves the possible growth in the value of your investment in the home. When you make monthly mortgage payments, some portion of the payment is going to the principal of the loan. As you "pay down" the principal you are building equity in your home. At the same time, your home may be appreciating as an asset, although property values can fluctuate as a function of the local economy of where you live, so you may not be able to control or influence this appreciation.

As you are making the own-versus-rent decision, you may

find that you will have saved money by owning when you put pencil to paper and tally all of your home expenses and tax considerations. In that case, the money you have freed up can be invested or used to pay down the principal faster. As you are considering the purchase of a home, you may discover that the rent you pay on an apartment might be less than the monthly cost of owning a home. This is because the cost of home ownership not only includes the mortgage payments and property taxes, but also the cost of insurance, repairs and maintenance. However, owning a home is usually not a short-term financial decision.

In addition to the rational, financial reasons to buying a home, there are considerable emotional reasons. An acquaintance of mine whose company provides relocation services for major corporations likes to talk about the engineers at one company he works with. When these engineers are transferred to a job in a distant city, my acquaintance helps them hunt for houses in the new location. The engineers go to great lengths to compare the various houses they are shown. First, they calculate the square footage versus the price to arrive at the cost per square foot. Then, they investigate heating and cooling costs, and break those down into costs per square foot. Then they painstakingly inspect the houses for defects. Then they walk through the rooms with a light meter to see how much sun shines in. Then they feed all this data into spreadsheet programs on their personal computers and generate sheaves of printouts.

But in the end, they buy the house they have a good feeling about. "Usually they just throw away their computer printouts so the numbers won't embarrass them," my friend says. "Sometimes they pretend they've made their decision on the basis of their spreadsheets. But it just ain't so. They end up buying on pure emotion."

Decisions to buy real estate for personal use are often colored by emotional considerations. If you're buying a house, which will probably be far and away the most expensive thing that you will ever buy, you ought to proceed fairly logically. But you may find it difficult to do so, because owning your own home has a special significance for most Americans that transcends dollars and cents.

If you're buying a house as an investment alternative to stocks and bonds, although it might be a very sound decision, it's also likely to be influenced by myths about the inevitability of making a fortune in real estate, myths that flowered for decades after World War II. In the 1980s, however, some home-owners discovered what securities investors had learned earlier: Trees don't grow to the sky. Housing prices stopped climbing and even dropped in many parts of the U.S. for the first time since the 1930s. While home prices started increasing again in many parts of the U.S. in the 1990s, the interruption in the escalation of housing prices provided the baby boom genera-tion with a valuable reminder that in housing, as in other mar-kets, price movements are not a one-way street.

House Shopping

Having decided to buy a home—either because of, or despite, what the figures show—you should still endeavor to keep a grip on yourself as you shop. You may well believe that you are buying a home to live in forever, and that your own likes and dislikes should therefore be the only factors in selecting one. But the odds are good that you are wrong about the for-ever part. Americans move a lot. Their families grow and they need more space. Or their grown children move out and they desire a little less "empty" space. They change jobs, get trans-ferred, get divorced, get bored. It could happen to you.

When you look at a house, therefore, you should consider it not only as something you are buying but also as something you might someday be selling. It may be hard to keep this in mind when you walk through the door of an old stone house and fall in love. This happens all the time. Real estate brokers talk about houses being sold from the instant the car carrying the would-be buyer first pulls into view of the property and he or she is immediately smitten by the place; it's love at first sight. There's nothing silly about this. People want to feel good about the place where they live, and a lot of that feeling derives from physical appearance and from intangible factors that people couldn't explain if they tried. But you should still make sure that you check the plumbing and everything else related to the house. Home inspection companies can often thoroughly review a home for sale and tell you if anything is wrong or in need of repair. And you should also make a careful inquiry regarding price levels in the local real estate market.

Before you start a search, you need to think about where you want to live and what you want to live in. Let's say that because of your job or your family or your allergies, you decide you want to live in Phoenix or Chicago, or wherever. But what exactly do you mean by that? Do you want to live in the city itself, or in the suburbs? What part of the city do you want to live in? Or what suburb? Do you need to be near a suburban train station? Do you want a specific school district? You need to zero in on an area or town.

You also need to think about the specific features you require in a house. How many rooms do you need? Do you want everything on one floor, or do you want a two-story home? What style do you like? And do you really want a house? You could buy an apartment, a town house, or a home in some kind of community with a clubhouse and a pool. You should investigate all the housing alternatives that you can afford. Many people who march into real estate offices announcing, "Now, don't try to show me any of those town-house things," have been pleasantly surprised when they looked into the economics—and lifestyle—associated with such developments.

Because every house is different and every neighborhood is different, you probably will need a guide, especially if you're moving into an area from elsewhere. Just as you can benefit from a good stockbroker to help you manage your securities investments, a good real estate agent will do wonders for your efforts to find a home.

Your real estate agent should be able to supply you with information on "comparables"—i.e., homes similar to the one you are considering that have recently been sold in the area. This information generally includes selling prices (and how they compare to original asking prices) and the length of time each home was on the market before it was sold. This data will tell you what types of homes—in terms of style, location, building size, and lot size—sell best in the area. It will also provide a good indication of the price that any home you're considering is likely to sell for. Some sellers, especially those who have just put their homes on the market, may not yet have gotten the message that they're asking too much. There is no ticker tape in the housing market, as there is on Wall Street, instantly broadcasting the prices of the most recent transactions. But armed with your "comparable" data, you will not be misled by the aspirations of the seller.

In addition to supplying you with market information, ideally your agent should offer firsthand knowledge of the communities you're looking into. An agent operating from an office two towns away may be eager to sell you something, but he or she is unlikely to be as helpful as one who works full-time in your target area. While local knowledge is helpful, on the other hand, it's also useful to work with an agent who has some sort of affiliation with real estate offices in other nearby communities. Many house hunters focus their search on a particularly well-known or desirable town, or area. But the prices in such communities may reflect their popularity. The result is frustration and disappointment as mere mortals learn that they cannot afford even the most humble bungalow in places like Beverly Hills. At this point, the names of other nearby towns need to be raised, and you will be ill-served by an agent who only sneers, "Oh, you wouldn't want to live *there!*" An enterprising agent with out-of-town affiliates can and should steer you to nearby communities that may be less prestigious because they're a few miles inland from the beach or a few stations farther out on the commuter line. These areas may offer perfectly fine homes at lower prices. As a buyer, you should bow to financial realities and be flexible.

While home ownership in the United States is the highest in history and the highest of any country in the world, you may have to be flexible with respect to the type of home you can buy and where you want to live. In some "hot" real estate markets, rising prices have put many homes out of the reach of those who thought a house and a yard were their birthright. Even if you think you can swing payments on a house you want, a lender may not agree. When you apply for a mortgage loan, the lender will look at several aspects of your financial profile before it will agree to make you a loan. Lenders will scrutinize your monthly income to see if you can afford to make the monthly mortgage payment. They will also review your credit history to see how you have handled other credit obligations in your life, everything from current and previous mortgages, to car loans, credit card debt and other personal loans. A title search will be conducted to insure that the home is free from claims from someone else. And lenders will send a home appraiser to inspect the house and determine whether it is worth what you are willing to pay for it. In the past few years, lenders have become more flexible and creative regarding some of their criteria, but you may still find that you have to make some compromises regarding the home you can buy, versus the home you might like to buy.

You can figure out how much you can afford to pay for a house by determining how much of a down payment you can make and how big a mortgage your income will let you carry. Most lenders will even calculate this for you and "prequalify" the loan, even before you have found a home you want. This "prequalification" is often provided in a letter or certificate and gives you added bargaining power with a seller as you shop for a home.

As you evaluate houses, keep in mind the old real estate dictum that you should buy the worst house in the best neighborhood you can afford. This doesn't necessarily mean that you should buy a henhouse behind a mansion (although that might not be too bad an idea); it does mean that a three-bedroom house in a neighborhood of five-bedroom houses will generally be worth relatively more and hold its value better than a five-bedroom house in a neighborhood of three-bedroom houses.

Sometimes the owners of much-improved houses learn this lesson to their despair. Let's say they purchased a three-bedroom house in a neighborhood of three-bedroom houses. Then they added a new bedroom wing, and a swimming pool, and parquet floors, and track lighting, and a wet bar, and a hot tub. They expect to get all their money back and maybe even more, when they go to sell. But that's not the way the real estate market works. Some improvements, such as extra rooms, do add value to a house, although even extra rooms may add less than expected if the house has become "over-built" compared to its neighbors. "Lifestyle" improvements—parquet floors and that sort of thing—rarely add as much to the selling price as they cost. A prospective buyer may loathe parquet or like the house but be concerned that his dog will drown in the hot tub. Even buyers who like the improvements will see the house primarily as a three-bedroom, two-bath (or whatever) and will be unwilling to pay much more for it than they would pay for any other three-bedroom, two-bath. This fact of real estate life often makes preexisting homes better bargains than brand-new homes, because everyone who lives in a house adds something to it; buyers of used homes get that something—landscaping, carpeting, whatever—at a discount. Of course, if you buy a home in a neighborhood where everyone is putting on lavish additions, it may not be bad to keep pace, since your home will be just as improved as everyone else's. It all comes back to knowing the community you are buying into.

After all your looking around, you may find that you like a house that others think has something "wrong" with it. Maybe it's a colonial in a town where ranches are popular, or it's far from schools (but you don't have kids), or it has relatively low ceilings (but you're just over five feet tall). Go ahead and buy it—but be sure the price is reduced to reflect those faults. Even if they don't seem like faults to you, they will to somebody else. When you buy a house that has low ceilings and is far from schools, you don't want to have to wait for a short, childless couple to sell to when you want to move on.

Mortgages

Once you have found the home you want, your shopping is still not done. It's time to shop for a mortgage. Most people can't pay cash for their house. And even if they could, it's probably a bad use of their money. For most people, getting a mortgage is the necessary and inevitable second step in the process of acquiring a house.

In the past, most people got their mortgage from a local bank or savings and loan association (S&L). You took a fixed-rate mortgage, usually for a 30-year term, and lived in this home for your entire adult life. At the end of the thirty years, you made the last payment, burned the mortgage, and you finally owned the home free and clear.

Much has changed today. People move much more frequently, sometimes to a different city for work-related reasons, but often just to "trade up" to a bigger home in the same town. As families grow, people want larger homes. When mortgage rates decline, many people refinance their mortgage loans. In response to this new pattern of home ownership and refinancing activity, financial institutions have developed new kinds of mortgage loans that offer more choices and more flexibility to meet different and varied lifestyles.

A fixed-rate mortgage is still the most popular mortgage today because it offers predictable monthly payments for the entire term of the loan. While the 30-year term is the length most often selected, other terms are also available—in particular, a 15-year term. With the latter, the monthly payments are higher, since the loan is paid off over a shorter term. However, 15-year fixed-rate mortgages save many thousands of dollars in interest payments.

Adjustable-rate mortgages are also appealing for many people. These mortgages have a 30-year payback term, but the interest rate is periodically adjusted in response to changes in some index. Adjustable-rate mortgages (ARMs) offer one of several different "caps," or maximum amounts that interest rates or monthly payments can be raised or lowered in a given period and over the life of the loan. You may also have a choice of the index that serves as the benchmark in adjusting your mortgage rate.

In recent years, many lenders, especially brokerage firms, have begun to offer specialized, "hybrid" mortgages. These may provide such features as the option of moving from fixed to adjustable rates, or paying interest but not principal for periods of time.

And finally, a relatively new mortgage product, available through securities firms, allows people to utilize their investment accounts so they don't have to come up with cash or sell investments to make a down payment on a home. This product is often used by parents to help an adult child purchase a home, since for many young adults the most difficult part of obtaining a mortgage is coming up with the down payment.

While most homeowners provide a sizable down payment on their mortgage, some lenders offer mortgage loans requiring down payments as low as 3 percent of the purchase price. However, these loans often come with higher interest rates.

Clearly, choosing among all of these mortgage products requires not only some careful calculations, but also consideration of how long you may think you will live in your home. No matter what kind of mortgage you hold, if interest rates become low enough, refinancing the loan is an option. However, refinancing may not be cost-effective every time rates decline a little bit, because lenders may charge up-front fees for making the new loan and impose sizable closing costs. Your current mortgage loan may even have a prepayment penalty, which is an additional fee charged if you pay your loan off before a stated time. These costs must be factored in before you can determine whether you will save money by refinancing at a lower rate.

Choosing a Lender

In shopping for a mortgage loan, you will find new types of mortgage lenders as well as many new types of mortgages. Banks and S&Ls have been joined by major securities firms, independent mortgage brokers and mortgage banking companies.

At any point in time, you will find some variation in the rates offered by competitive lenders. Shop around and read all the fine print in the deals. Some lenders advertise great rates but have hidden costs that escalate the true cost of borrowing. Pay attention to points, fees and closing costs. You can get a quick fix on local and national lender deals by looking at rate monitors in your newspaper's real estate section, usually on Sundays. Your real estate agent should be able to advise you about mortgage lenders in the area, and some real estate agents are even affiliated with financial institutions that make mortgage loans. You should ask your stockbroker if his or her firm makes mortgage loans; many firms do. Finally, the Internet is an excellent resource, as several Web sites offer mortgage loans from a wide range of lenders, providing easy comparison of rates and terms as well as the convenience of on-line applications.

Changes in interest rates can have a significant impact on the prices of homes. During periods of higher interest rates, many people may be dissuaded from buying a home. This decreases the demand for homes and forces sellers to offer homes at lower prices. When interest rates go down, conversely, the demand for homes can go up, as can their prices. Nonetheless, even in high-rate environments, many would-be homebuyers decide they are better off buying rather than waiting; they may take a shorter-term ARM loan and bet that they can refinance in the future when rates decline.

If it makes sense for you to buy a home, there is no particular interest-rate environment that is necessarily better or worse in which to shop for one. The important thing to remember is that you must shop around—for the right home, the right lender and the right loan. This will take more time than if you accepted the first loan offered by the first lender you meet to buy the first home you feel good about. But you could save yourself thousands of dollars for each hour you extend the search.

Home Equity Loans

Your home is both an investment and not an investment. You generally buy a house because you like it and want to live in it. But when buying a home, you need to be aware of its current market value and also have some idea of its potential future value. While you may purchase more than one home in your adult life, you'll probably find it inconvenient to buy and sell homes on a frequent basis, as if they were shares of stock.

Because your home is likely to be the single largest purchase and single largest investment of your life, it should play a central role in all of your long-term financial planning. In many ways, you can let your home function as a sort of automatic savings account. As you pay down your mortgage loan, your equity will grow. In addition, your home's value may be appreciating, so you will be building wealth.

As you build equity in your home, you have a couple of financial choices. You can let it sit there, and make a good profit if and when you decide to sell your home. Or you can borrow against this equity, using it to secure a short-term loan. Loan products that allow you to borrow against the equity in your home are called home equity loans and home equity lines of credit.

With a home equity loan, you get an upfront sum of money, the interest rate is usually fixed and your monthly payments are predictable. With a home equity line of credit, you get a predetermined credit limit; a rate usually tied to the prime rate and a checkbook. Every time you write a check on the line, your credit limit decreases and every payment of loan principal you make increases the credit limit. The monthly payments are usually based on a percentage of the total balance, much like credit cards, and some lenders simply require interest-only monthly payments with a balloon payment of principal due at the end of the loan term (usually 10 or 15 years).

Thus, if you have a temporary need for cash to remodel your home, pay a tax bill, pay off credit card debt, pay for your daughter's wedding or college education, a home equity loan is a good source. It may make sense to think of a home equity line of credit as an "emergency reserve," accessing it when necessary to leave your investments and savings undisturbed. If you're earning 7 percent on bonds, leave it there and borrow at under 6 percent to pay for that new kitchen. The only thing you can't use home equity proceeds for is to purchase, trade or carry marketable securities.

Home equity loans come with an important caveat, however. If you don't pay the loan back, as with any mortgage loan, the lender can foreclose on your house and use the proceeds to pay off the loan. For that reason, home equity loans or lines of credit should be taken seriously and used with caution. Nonetheless, when used wisely, this is an attractive source of funds because it is a relatively inexpensive way to borrow. Since the loan is secured by your home, this represents less risk to the lender, who charges a lower interest rate than on other unsecured forms of credit (like credit cards). Moreover, since home equity debt is a mortgage loan, the interest is usually tax deductible, subject to some rules and restrictions. In the higher tax brackets, the after-tax cost of borrowing for a 9 percent home equity loan could be below 6 percent. That's a pretty cheap way to borrow.

For most people, a home is the place they live and raise their family. But your home can also play a significant role in building your overall wealth.

"Real" Real Estate Investments

Beyond your home, other real estate investments beckon. These come in the form of both "hands-on" investments in land and buildings and "hands-off" investments that resemble stocks and bonds in that they're pieces of paper, but they're linked to land and buildings.

"Hands-on" Real Estate

"Hands-on" real estate investments—those in which you become an owner of, or mortgage holder on, specific buildings— offer their own distinct advantages and disadvantages. Whether they appeal to you will depend as much on your personality as on your investment goals. If you are a real estate kind of person, you may find such investments especially rewarding.

We're not talking about going out and buying Rockefeller Center. But consider the case of a man I met in Connecticut. Let's call him Andrew. Andrew was a resident of Hartford who found himself with some money to invest a few years ago. At the time, Andrew was living in a rental apartment in an old section of town. His rent was an exceedingly reasonable $300 a month, but the place was getting shabby, and he was not inclined to fix it up. When a visiting woman friend remarked on some peeling wallpaper under a leak, Andrew explained, "I live by two rules: Don't eat white bread, and no capital improvements in a rented place."

To improve his housing situation, Andrew had the choice of either breaking rule number two, or renting a nicer apartment at two to three times his present rent, or buying something. Looking around his own neighborhood, which is home to many poor people but has a solid core of blue-collar families and owner-occupied homes, he found a six-apartment building offered at $106,000. He put $40,000 down (money he might otherwise have used to buy stocks) and took out a fixed-rate, twenty-year, 9 percent mortgage. His monthly payment was $593.82.

The building Andrew bought had been haphazardly maintained by absentee landlords for decades, which was one reason the price was so low. Andrew was aware of the building's poor condition—he had hired an independent engineer to prepare a detailed report on the building before he bought it—but he knew it was structurally sound and could be improved, and he was prepared to do much of the work himself.

Andrew moved into the building and began to renovate the exterior, learning about home repair as he went along (and accumulating a fine set of tax-deductible tools). A gang of teenagers whom he initially wanted to keep out of his yard by building a fence ended up pitching in and helping him build it. Skilled carpenters who lived in the neighborhood assisted with other jobs at reduced rates. Some of Andrew's neighbors were inspired by his example to fix up their own homes, which in turn increased the value of Andrew's building.

Andrew renovated the apartments in the building one at a time, as they became vacant, and he raised the rents accordingly. When he first bought the building, he was charging as little as $265 a month (plus heat) for an apartment. After renovation, the same apartments went for over $500 and were considered bargains by their new tenants.

Andrew occasionally had tenant trouble—he had to evict one woman who fell $1,500 behind in her rent—but he found that the least desirable tenants generally had such chaotic personal lives that they eventually moved out of their own accord. There was little resentment of the modest rent increases he imposed on old tenants because the increases always followed actual improvements to the apartments, and the tenants could see Andrew himself working to make those improvements. One tenant was happy to pay $80 a month more largely to have his old pull light chains replaced by mid-twentieth century wall switches.

Four years after he bought the place, Andrew had spent an additional $48,000, but his monthly rental income substantially exceeded his monthly payments on his mortgage and building improvement loans (and he had substantial tax savings as well). He had received one unsolicited offer of $190,000 for the building, and his next-door neighbor had sold his (smaller) building for $220,000. Andrew held on to his property for two more years. Then he sold out for $320,000, and a lease in the building.

Investments like Andrew's have been profitable for many Americans. Owner-occupied two- and three-family houses are common sights in many cities. By becoming small-time landlords, many people have been able to acquire homes they could not otherwise have afforded. The rental income often falls short of meeting the total building costs, but it does make a substantial contribution, putting the owner-landlord in the happy position of building up their equity with somebody else's money. (Moreover, when they put a new roof on their home, half the cost is a tax-deductible business expense.)

Investors who prefer not to be their tenant's neighbors, or who have grander things in mind, can buy rental houses or small apartment buildings in which they do not live themselves. They can also buy pretty much any other kind of building that comes in modest sizes: a store or warehouse, for example, or a building with a half dozen offices that can be rented out. Whatever the nature of the property, however, those who do best with such investments tend to have some things in common with owner-occupants like Andrew:

- They buy in territory they know. They live near, if not in, their investment properties, and they are able to choose

wisely because of their knowledge of which neighborhoods are solid and which are not, and which depressed
neighborhoods seem to be starting to turn around. These
investors supplement their general knowledge of the community by carefully inspecting many properties before
they buy. (Although he already lived in the neighborhood himself, Andrew called on other property owners
before he bought to ask about their plans for their buildings and their experiences with tenants.)

- They are prepared to work at their investments. Even
if they don't intend to fix up their properties themselves,
they carefully supervise the workers they hire. They also
tend to manage their own properties—advertising for tenants, screening potential tenants, and responding to
tenant problems and complaints. They could hire a management company to do all this for them, but a management fee could eat up their entire profit, and an outside
manager might not work as hard as they would.

The rewards for all this effort come from several sources:

Rental Income

Every month, while money is going out for mortgage payments, tax bills, repairs, and utilities, money is also coming in.
(This assumes that the owner has been successful not only in
finding tenants but also in collecting rent from them.) Although the rental income from small buildings will probably
not cover the owner's expenses at first, in the long run rents
often go up faster than the cost of owning a building (especially
if the owner has a fixed-rate mortgage). In the meantime, the
owner may still show a profit on the place, because of:

Tax Breaks

Interest payments on mortgage loans (and other loans to
improve the property as well) are deductible on the owner's

federal income tax. So are property taxes and all other expenses incurred in maintaining rental property (like Andrew's new tools). Most important, there is also a deduction for depreciation. The IRS operates on the assumption that a building, any building, is deteriorating and losing value over time. On this basis, the owner is allowed to deduct a portion of the building's original cost every year as a loss due to depreciation. This loss is a paper loss. Even if the building is crumbling, it's not necessarily taking any actual cash out of the owner's pocket in doing so—and it may actually be growing in value, depending on where it is located.

Mortgage interest deductions, depreciation, and other tax issues related to real estate are governed by some very complex regulations. So an investor needs to talk to his or her tax advisor about the tax treatment of many aspects of real estate expenditures and income.

Leverage and Appreciation

Leverage in real estate results from the fact that most people do not buy property with cash. If you buy a $200,000 property, you may put down as little as $20,000 and take a mortgage for the rest. If the property then proceeds to appreciate 10 percent a year for two years, you can sell it for $240,000. This is a profit not of 20 percent but of 200 percent on your original investment of $20,000. (This is a simplified example, since it would have cost you something to own the building for two years and to sell it; even so, leverage vastly increases your profit potential.)

But leverage can also work against you. If you go to sell your $200,000 property and find that you can get only $200,000 for it, and meanwhile you've spent $20,000 to maintain it, then you've lost 100 percent of your original investment, even though your property is still worth what you paid for it. If property values have actually gone down, your situation will be catastrophic.

Historically, property values in many areas have generally

gone up, at the rate of inflation, if not faster. During the boom real estate years of the late 1970s, when real estate values zoomed way beyond inflation, leverage and appreciation worked together to make many real estate investors rich. An investor might buy a $100,000 property, say, with a $10,000 down payment and a $90,000 mortgage. A year or so later, when the property was worth $120,000, he would take out an additional $20,000 loan against its increased value. He would use that $20,000 to make down payments on another property or two. When their value increased, he would repeat the process. From a single $10,000 down payment, he might end up with dozens of properties.

As long as property values soared, this was a very profitable game. Like all Great Truths in the past, however, the proposition that "you can't lose money buying real estate" attracted swirling mobs of adherents—and then ceased being true. Property values leveled off. Investors who didn't get off the escalator in time were hurt.

While appreciation has slowed since the 1970s, modest increases in real estate prices, abetted by leverage (and the natural equity buildup that ensues simply by making mortgage payments), can still enable a smart investor to borrow against one property to buy another and thus build up a modest real estate empire, albeit at a slower pace than in the high-flying 1970s.

Nevertheless, there are no guaranteed fortunes in real estate. The market can turn sour. Tenants can turn surly. And there are some additional drawbacks to real estate that do not apply to stocks and bonds:

- Real estate is not liquid. You can almost always sell a share of stock. You may not always be able to find a buyer for a building.
- The real estate selling commission is a stiff one, typically 6 percent (and 10 percent on raw land). On a $100,000 house on which you have made a 10 percent down pay-

ment, the $6,000 commission amounts to a whooping 60 percent of your original investment. You have to make a pretty good profit when you sell to overcome that.

- In real estate, depreciation is not just an accounting concept; buildings do fall apart. Maintenance is a constant and costly necessity and must be carefully calculated in any estimate of the rate of return on a real estate investment. You can get lucky and have a furnace that lasts forever, but you can also be unlucky and have pipes that keep leaking.

Owning investment real estate is much more like running a business than what most people think of as "investing." You don't sit and read reports; you walk around basements with flashlights and buy things in hardware stores. That's why making direct investments in real estate is an acquired taste. Some people love it, and some don't. To determine if you're suited to invest in real estate, ask yourself if you have the desire and the skills needed to take care of buildings. Sure, you can always hire somebody to fix most anything, but paying someone else will eat into the return on your investment.

You also need to be good at negotiating with lots of people—suppliers and repair people, tenants and city officials.

Another requirement is a cushion of extra cash. When you buy stock, nobody asks you for more money. But when you buy a building, you may want or need to pump in additional money. Yes, you have rental income and insurance, but suddenly you need to buy this or that or hire someone to take care of something. You'd better be able to foot those bills.

There is a certain satisfaction in buying a stock at $10 a share and watching it grow to $20 over the next few years, but for some people there is far greater satisfaction in locating a run-down building, negotiating its purchase, redesigning it, fixing it up, finding tenants, negotiating leases, lobbying the city council on rent control, learning about the tenants' problems, attending a tenant's son's bar mitzvah, fixing leaks, doing the books, watching the neighborhood turn around—and then doing it again.

If you would like to be this actively involved in your investments, then look to real estate. If reading the financial pages and making an occasional telephone call to your broker is involvement enough for you, then maybe you don't want to be a real estate tycoon after all.

"Hands-off" Real Estate Investments

If you like the idea of investing in real estate but don't want to have anything to do with actual buildings, then you should think about "hands-off" real estate investments—i.e., securities. Just as mortgage-backed securities made it possible for individual investors to be mortgage holders, other securities have made it possible for the average middle-class family to be the proud owner of investment real estate without getting any phone calls from tenants demanding more heat in the winter.

Real Estate Investment Trusts (REITs)

REITs are similar in concept to mutual funds that invest in stocks and bonds. REITs raise money from investors and invest it in a portfolio of buildings. Most REITs actually buy buildings, although some make mortgage loans to buildings, and some have both debt and equity investments in real estate. REIT shares are listed on stock exchanges, and if you call your stockbroker—not a real estate agent—he or she can buy or sell REIT shares for you as readily as stocks and bonds.

Like mutual funds, REITs provide diversification and professional management. Also like mutual funds, REITs make it possible for small investors to own a piece of something they couldn't acquire on their own—in this case, ownership of skyscrapers, shopping malls, and major hotels. From the point of view of the investor, REITs transform an illiquid investment (real estate) into a liquid one (securities). While it can take months for the REIT itself to buy and sell buildings, the REITs investors can buy and sell their shares in the REIT with a phone call.

REITs went through a couple of boom-and-bust cycles in the 1970s and 1980s, but they were resurrected in the 1990s. At year-end 1999, the National Association of Real Estate Investment Trusts counted some 203 REITs, with a total market capitalization of more than $124 billion. These included 167 equity REITs, which invest directly in property; 26 mortgage REITs, which invest in loans on real estate; and 10 hybrids, which had both equity and debt interests in real estate. A number of REITs specialize in specific types of properties—hotels, or office buildings, or apartments—or in specific geographic regions.

REITs are not "pure" real estate plays. The share price reflects not only the value of the real estate owned by the REIT but also trends in the stock market. However, they can get you close to the real estate market without getting your hands dirty.

Limited Partnerships

Instead of pooling your money with thousands of other investors in a REIT, you could join with a smaller group of investors in a real estate limited partnership. These are real estate ventures in which a general partner takes money put up by limited partners (i.e., you) and invests in a portfolio of buildings. Partnerships may purchase apartment buildings, office buildings, shopping centers, warehouses, or anything else, and the general partner will take care of managing and maintaining the holdings. The partnership seeks to provide its investors with a substantial cash flow (from rents on the properties) as well as profits from appreciation of the properties when they are sold several years down the road. Of course, the general partner gets a nice share of the profits for its efforts.

In contrast to REITs, limited partnerships often require

substantial initial investments. They are also illiquid: You're signing up for a number of years, and it can be difficult or costly to get your money back ahead of schedule. Moreover, while REITs send you a simple Form 1099 showing you how to report your investment results for tax purposes, limited partnerships can involve some fairly complex tax issues. In fact, before the tax reform legislation in the mid-1980s, a major appeal of limited partnerships in real estate and other areas was their ability to serve as a tax shelter.

These days, limited partnerships, whether in real estate or other fields, are designed to enable small groups of investors to capitalize on attractive opportunities that the general partner ferrets out. Real estate limited partnerships have had their ups and downs, so you should thoroughly examine the general partner's investment intentions and previous track record. Real estate limited partnerships differ from REITs not only in that they involve smaller numbers of investors, but also because they are subject to less regulation than REITs, which are listed on an exchange and sold to the general public. That's why you should talk to your accountant, lawyer, and stockbroker about any real estate investment partnership you're considering and find out as much as you can about its sponsors.

Real Estate vs. Other Investments

You don't need to buy coveralls and a toolbox to invest in REITs and limited partnerships. Here, the principal task facing you is to decide what you think the outlook is for real estate vis-à-vis other investments. Owning a home has much to do with your lifestyle needs and aspirations. Investing in real estate that you're not going to live in requires a careful evaluation of the real estate in the context of all of your potential investment choices.

Whether you're interested in gaining exposure to real estate by owning bricks and mortar or by purchasing pieces of paper, you have to assess what return you think real estate can deliver and how that stacks up against what you might get in some other investment. But real estate offers more than the potential for attractive returns. Real estate often marches to a different drummer than stocks and bonds, so you get additional diversification in your holdings by investing in some real estate. If real estate is zigging while your stocks are zagging, on balance you may be better off.

Remember your home is your castle, but it's also your biggest single investment. It can generate returns as well as memories, and you should keep both things in mind. Beyond that, you should remain aware of the opportunities that real estate investments can offer, whether these investments are of the hands-on or hands-off variety.

CHAPTER 9

LIFE INSURANCE

Principles of Insurance

A while ago I spoke to an elderly widow who asked me to look over her financial affairs. It turned out that they were quite rosy: She had a net worth of more than $600,000 and living expenses of about $30,000 a year. Her assets included substantial amounts of stocks and bonds as well as savings and checking accounts containing more than $35,000.

And then there was her life insurance policy. Every year, year after year, she was paying a few hundred dollars for an old policy with a death benefit of $25,000. The cost was modest, but I could see no reason for her to be spending anything at all on life insurance. What did she need it for?

"That's to bury me," she said.

Oh. I cast my eyes down the list of her assets. "We could sell a few dozen shares of Ford Motor Company to bury you," I said. I glanced at her latest bank statement. "We could just write the funeral director a check."

This had never occurred to her. She had the idea that her life insurance policy—and only her life insurance policy—was guaranteeing that her body would not someday be tossed into a mass grave in a potter's field. This was "pocket accounting" in the extreme. The fact that she had accumulated enough assets to pay for a catered funeral at a Ritz-Carlton Hotel, if she wanted one, had not changed her old way of thinking.

The purchase of life insurance, like every other financial decision, must be approached with a clear perspective. You probably *do* need to have life insurance, and you may well need a great deal more of it than you think. But you should clearly understand both the reasons for purchasing insurance and the costs associated with it. Any money diverted from earning the highest possible return may be costing you a great deal.

Insurance companies may seem to be gamblers since their business is based on an endless series of bets with individuals as to when they will die. Policyholders who sign up, pay a premium or two, and then promptly kick the bucket "win" their bets; the company pays their beneficiaries more than the policyholder ever paid the company. Policyholders who live to a ripe old age "lose" their bets; they may pay more in premiums than their beneficiaries will ever get back. The insurance companies have a nice edge in this process, in that everyone who buys a policy works very hard to lose his or her bet with the company.

The insurance company generally comes out ahead no matter who wins in any individual case because mortality statistics are not random but highly predictable. It's impossible to know precisely when Sally Smith, age thirty-six, will go to meet her maker. But assemble a pool of ten thousand thirty-six-year-old women, and insurance company statisticians, guided by years of death records, can predict with a high degree of accuracy how many of those women will die next year, and the year after that, and so on. An insurance company cannot determine *which* of its policyholders will die every year, but it can determine, with a fair degree of accuracy, *how many* of them will. So it's a fairly easy matter for the company to set its rates at a level that will cover all the death benefits it will have to pay and also generate a profit—barring an unforeseeable mass calamity. (And insurance companies specifically exclude death caused by many mass calamities from coverage.)

So the insurance companies are able to make a buck and stay in business. And this is a good thing, because, by providing a mechanism by which individuals share the financial risks of premature death, they perform a valuable service. The affordable sums of money they collect from many individuals form a pool that is redistributed to families of deceased policyholders—families that might be facing financial catastrophe were it not for life insurance.

This is the primary purpose of life insurance, and the only reason most people should have life insurance: to protect their dependents from a major decline in their standard of living if the policyholder dies before he or she has had enough time to accumulate a substantial estate. Someday, if you have the ability and discipline to adopt and maintain the kind of investment plan we have discussed in this book, you will not need life insurance. You will have achieved financial serenity, and, when you die, your dependents will be able to live nicely on the assets you leave behind. (Although, if your assets are substantial but not liquid, you may want to retain some life insurance to help your heirs pay estate taxes.)

Even if you have embarked on a steady investment program, however, you may die before you have time to reach your goal. As a young or middle-aged working person, you may still be years away from it. If you died, your family would be in trouble. Life insurance provides an instant shortcut to the goal you did not have time to reach. You need this guarantee to protect your family, and you cannot get it from anything but life insurance. Before you begin any other kind of investment program, therefore, you must be sure that your insurance needs are met.

How Much Do You Need?

What are your insurance needs?

Unfortunately, there isn't any pat answer to that question. There used to be various rules of thumb. For example, people said you ought to have life insurance equal to seven times the breadwinner's annual salary. But these rules were generally predicated on the "Leave It to Beaver" model household, the one with a working husband, a homemaker spouse, and two children. These days, there seems to be much more variety in family life: There are lots of two-income households, some with children and some without. And there are all those blended households with his kids, her kids, and their kids, plus the kids living with the former spouses. How much insurance do you need? Enough to meet all of the financial obligations and commitments you have to your survivors. Every case is unique, and you can determine your own insurance needs only by making some fairly extensive calculations about your personal situation.

For starters, your family will need a lump sum to pay for your "last expenses": the funeral, medical bills not covered by health insurance, and other things related to your departure. Then, on an ongoing basis, your family will probably need in the range of 60 to 75 percent of the income you are no longer earning to maintain themselves in the style to which you got them accustomed. (They will no longer need 100 percent of your income, because you won't be around to run up any expenses and because you were presumably saving some of your income and you don't need to replace that.) In making these calculations, bear in mind that your family will need a big boost in income (or an extra lump sum) if you have children to put through college. Afterward, income needs will be less, as your children start to earn their own livings. And still less money will be needed when your surviving spouse reaches retirement age and presumably begins to receive a pension and Social Security.

In short, your insurance needs will be represented by a sum of money that will provide for all your family's onetime expenses and still leave enough to generate the income they will need over the long term. That sum must be increased to allow for inflation; and it may be reduced if your family is prepared to gradually dip into the principal instead of just living off the interest. Any life insurance agent (many of whom are armed nowadays with laptop computers and programs for working up these figures) will be only too pleased to help you with your calculations.

The number you come up with as your family's insurance requirement is likely to be several hundred thousand dollars or more, but don't be alarmed. Not all of that money will have to be provided by life insurance. Depending on the size of your contributions to Social Security over the years and the number of dependents in your family, your surviving spouse and children may be eligible for Social Security benefits of $2,000 a month or more (although benefits may stop when your youngest child reaches age eighteen and will be cut back before that if your spouse is working). Whatever Social Security benefits you receive will reduce your need for insurance by the amount required to produce that income. Your insurance needs will also be reduced by your spouse's future income potential (although that may be offset by child-care and housekeeping costs) and possible support from doting grandparents or other relatives. Finally, there is the important matter of the wealth you have already accumulated. Whatever your family will inherit from you can be deducted from the amount of insurance you need.

Whatever your final conclusion about your insurance needs, it is important to review your calculations on a regular basis. Circumstances will change. Your son will finally get a job and become self-supporting. But your daughter may decide to go to medical school and need your financial help for the next half dozen years. Your investments may have grown as the years have gone by, so your insurance needs may decrease. On the other hand, at age forty-five you may become the proud— and surprised—parents of triplets. Congratulations—and call your insurance agent.

By the way, you need insurance on a spouse who is not working outside the home or generating any income. Full–time homemakers may serve as child-care providers, house-keepers, cooks, and more. Hiring people to fill those jobs is likely to be surprisingly expensive. Insurance can provide the money to pay for it.

The insurance needs of childless couples may be less obvious. The surviving spouse may have a good job, but many two-income couples have sizable financial commitments, like mortgage payments or college loans, that a surviving spouse cannot easily handle alone. And what if you are single, with no entangling financial alliances and no dependents at present or on the horizon? You may want some insurance to spare your parents or distant relatives the burden of "last expenses." Beyond that, you probably don't need insurance at all.

Remember that the amount of life insurance you have is not a measure of your importance or your self-esteem. If there is no one that you need to provide for financially, you don't really need life insurance. But if you're helping to support someone, then you'd better figure out just how much insurance you need to ensure that their lives will go on without financial hardship, even if your life is abruptly ended.

Young people are often urged to buy insurance because it is much cheaper to buy a policy at age twenty-five, say, than at age forty (for the very good reason that a twenty-five-year-old is less likely to die than a forty-year-old). But the cheapness argument can be misleading. If you are buying term insurance, on which the premium increases as you get older, you will pay the same premium at age forty as any other forty-year-old, no matter how long you have had your policy. If you are buying whole life insurance, on which the premium never changes, at twenty-five you will indeed be paying a lower premium than a person who takes out the policy at age forty, but depending on the interest rate paid by the insurance company, you may be sacrificing the money you could have earned by investing that money elsewhere over the life of the policy. Even if the policy really is cheap, why buy it if you don't need it?

About the only good argument for buying insurance when you're young and without dependents is that many companies offer policies that guarantee you the right to buy more insurance later at standard rates, even if your health has deteriorated. If you eventually acquire both dependents and health problems, this guarantee could be valuable. But even then, you may find ways to get coverage without having spent a great deal of money ensuring your ability to get insurance.

Your Insurance Options

Once you have established your insurance needs, the next step is to determine how much insurance you already have. Many employees get group life insurance as a fringe benefit from their jobs. If your insurance needs are modest, such a policy may be all that you require. You may also have, or be eligible to buy, inexpensive group insurance through organizations of which you are a member. These days, everybody from the Benevolent and Protective Order of Elks to the B'nai B'rith and your college alumni association is selling life insurance.

If these policies don't cover your needs, then you should buy more insurance, and buy it promptly. As you begin to shop around, you will quickly discover that insurance companies, securities firms, banks, and others who sell life insurance offer three main varieties:

Term Insurance

For younger people, this is generally the cheapest kind of life insurance in terms of actual cash outlay on a year-to-year basis. As such, it is often the policy of choice for young families with large insurance needs and modest incomes.

Term insurance is "pure" insurance. It has no savings or investment component, unlike whole life and universal life, which are described later. With term insurance, insurance company statisticians figure out the probability of your death and set a rate that, when large numbers of people buy insurance, covers all the benefits that will have to be paid out.

Term insurance is often sold on an "annual renewable" basis. Every year the policy expires and you have the option of renewing. But every year the policy will be more expensive. At age twenty-five, you may pay little more than $1 for each $1,000 of coverage you get. (Women always pay less than men, because they live longer, and many companies offer special rates to nonsmokers, because they live longer too.) At age forty, you may pay almost $2 per $1,000. At age sixty, you may pay more than $7 per $1,000. As you enter old age, the cost of term insurance eventually becomes prohibitively high, but you may no longer need insurance by then.

Term insurance can also be purchased for longer terms— typically five or ten years—during which the annual premium will remain level. Since your risk of dying rises each year, the actual cost of insuring you also rises inexorably every year as you age. But with these extended-term policies, the insurance company manages to keep the premium level by charging you more than is required during the early years and holding that money to help pay the amounts required in later years, when your probability of dying has risen. If you renew the policy when it expires after five or ten years, the annual premium will generally jump up.

Another variation on term insurance is "decreasing term," where you pay the same premium every year, but the size of the death benefit goes down. Mortgage insurance, which many lenders require home buyers to purchase, is actually a form of decreasing-term insurance. The face value of the policy decreases year by year, in step with the remaining balance on the mortgage. If the borrower dies, an amount sufficient to pay off the mortgage instantly becomes available. (Similar "credit insurance" policies are available to pay off other kinds of indebtedness.)

These policies protect the borrower's family, but they also protect the mortgage lender. If you have the option not to buy mortgage insurance, it is often a good idea to opt out. Instead of buying a separate policy earmarked for your mortgage—a clear case of "pocket accounting"—you should include your family's housing expenses in your calculation of your total insurance needs and make sure these expenses are covered by whatever policy you do buy. You may end up getting the equivalent of mortgage insurance at a lower rate (a $200,000 policy costs less than two $100,000 policies). Moreover, your survivors will have the choice of paying off the mortgage immediately or simply continuing to make monthly payments. If you've got a mortgage with a low interest rate, there is no reason to rush out and pay it off. An insurance beneficiary might well be better off continuing to make the monthly payments while investing the rest of the insurance proceeds at an attractive return.

Regular term policies are offered with a wide range of options. Two common and valuable ones are the automatic right of renewal up to age sixty-five or seventy, regardless of what happens to your health, and the right to convert your policy to whole life insurance, again regardless of the future state of your health. Another potentially valuable option is known as a "waiver of premium." This provides that your insurance will continue in force, with no further premium payments from you, if you become disabled.

One option you don't want is "double indemnity." This doubles the death benefit if you die as a result of an accident or violence instead of disease. There is, however, generally no reason why your dependents' needs should be any greater if you are killed by a runaway oxcart than if you die of double pneumonia. The extra charge for double indemnity is better spent buying a slightly larger policy without that feature. Similarly, you should avoid "accidental death and dismemberment" policies unless you are planning to fall off a cliff soon. Such policies are cheap, but they pay nothing to your survivors if you die of natural causes, as most people do. Remember that the cause of your death may be interesting to the coroner, but not to your bill collectors.

Whatever you buy, shop around. Term insurance rates vary widely from company to company. You may also find that if you have any kind of medical problem, some companies may insist on charging you extra, while others will not. To learn more about prices, you can ask representatives of various insurance companies, and you can also turn to on-line services that will help you search for the lowest price quote. You should also follow up on the brochures you receive from fraternal organizations, alumni associations, and assorted other clubs that offer life insurance to their members.

Whole Life Insurance

Whole life insurance is generally more expensive than term insurance, at least in the short run. Whole life is also known as "permanent" life insurance because the coverage doesn't expire as long as you keep paying the annual premium. And unlike it does with term, the premium never increases; it is fixed for life at the time you buy the policy. (The younger you are when you buy, the lower the premium will be.) Since the premiums are held level while the actual cost of insurance increases as you age, you are in effect overpaying during the early years of your policy. Some of the money from those early overpayments goes to pay the higher actual costs of insuring you later on, and some goes to build up "cash value."

The cash value of a policy gradually increases, and it will be paid to you if you cancel the insurance. (It is not added to the face value of the policy if you die, however.) It takes a number of years for the cash value to build up to a substantial sum. Once it does, you may draw on it to pay your premiums. You may also borrow it out of the policy at a low interest rate, possibly to invest it elsewhere at a higher rate. You don't ever have to repay such loans, but the amount you have borrowed will be deducted from the death benefit paid to your beneficiary when you die.

One common variation on whole life requires you to pay premiums for only a limited number of years. With a "limited-payment life" policy, you pay for a set period (usually ten years, twenty years, or until you turn sixty-five), after which the policy is "paid up" and remains in force with no additional payments. The premiums on these policies are, not surprisingly, higher than those on comparable amounts of ordinary whole life insurance policies. So if your insurance budget is limited, you may obtain more insurance coverage, particularly during the years you need it most, if you choose other options.

Some whole life policies, finally, are known as "participating" policies and pay "dividends" to policyholders if the insurance company's investments (which it buys with the premium money it collects from policyholders) perform well. These dividends, which are received on a tax-free basis by policyholders, enable them to share some of the benefits reaped by the company during periods of good investment returns. However, participating policies generally charge higher premiums than "nonparticipating" policies. Thus, the payment of dividends may or may not proceed to make the participating policies cheaper.

Universal Life Insurance

For many years, life insurance agents encouraged consumers to buy whole life insurance instead of term because of the savings function of the cash value buildup in whole life policies. And for many years consumers were satisfied to hand over annual premiums to insurance companies and see their cash values (possibly augmented by dividends) pile up at modest rates of return. However, many consumers began to notice that they could earn a much higher return on their savings elsewhere than in a whole life insurance policy. It seemed smarter to buy term insurance and invest the difference—the amount you were saving by not buying whole life—in something that offers a higher rate of return.

Insurance companies responded to these changes in the investment marketplace by introducing "universal life," which, in a sense, enables consumers to buy insurance protection and receive the return earned by funds they have invested within the context of a single life insurance contract.

Part of the premium paid into a universal life policy is

allocated to pay for term insurance on a permanent renewing basis. Part goes to pay administrative fees and to give the insurance company its profit. But the rest goes into a cash value fund, which functions as an investment and offers rates of return competitive with many other investments. A minimum rate of return, typically 4 or 4.5 percent, is guaranteed, but the actual rate paid will depend upon the performance of the insurance company's investments.

Whatever the rate of return, no income tax is due until the money is paid out. This is true of the cash value funds in whole life insurance policies as well. Since tax reform legislation in the mid-1980s put an end to many "tax shelters," the so-called "inside buildup" of money in an insurance policy is one of the few remaining ways to accumulate funds on a tax-deferred basis. Money held in an insurance account compounds tax-free in the same fashion as assets in 401(k) plans, annuities, and certain other retirement plans.

Universal life policies offer the additional advantage of being extremely flexible. It's easy to change the amount of the death benefit or to increase or decrease the amount of the annual premium. You may increase the premium if you wish to build up your investment fund or decrease it to as low as the bare minimum required to pay for your insurance coverage (an amount approximately equivalent to a term insurance premium).

One variation on universal life offered by some insurance companies is variable universal life, which allows policyholders to decide how their cash value funds will be invested. In ordinary universal life, the cash value funds of all policyholders are pooled and invested as the insurance company sees fit. In variable universal, each policyholder specifies which of several mutual funds he wants his cash value invested in; depending upon how well he chooses, his return may be higher or lower than that of other policyholders.

It's not easy to select the best universal life policy. Cash values in different policies build up at different rates, depending not only on the rate of return being earned by each insurance company but also on how that company chooses to deduct its charges for administration and profit. The best way to compare two policies is to look at their projected cash buildups—at the same projected interest rate—some years down the road.

Some companies pay higher interest rates than others and make a great point of it in their sales promotion. But be careful. The woods are full of young companies promising high rates of return. To deliver those high returns, however, the companies may be forced to invest in riskier securities than companies promising lower returns. Remember that with universal life, you will be sharing that risk. Some companies promising a high return may be practicing a sort of "bait-and-switch" tactic. A young company with few policies on its books can afford to pay an above-market rate of return for a couple of years and absorb the loss, because it is not paying that return on very many policies. After it has attracted a load of new customers, it may slowly drop its rate of return to the level of other companies, or even below that level.

If you already have a whole life policy, you may be tempted to switch to universal life. Whether this is a good move or not will depend on a number of factors, including the specifics of your current policy and your age. If your whole life policy has been in force for a number of years, it may finally be accumulating cash value at a rapid rate. You may be better off keeping it in force, paying the annual premium, and then borrowing the amount of the premium (and perhaps more) to buy universal life.

To determine the best course for you, you'll have to go over the details of your old policy and the proposed new one. To make the hearing fair, you may want to talk to two insurance professionals—the one who wants to sell you universal life and the one who originally sold you the whole life policy. You should be careful about canceling your old policy—that can create tax bills—but you could exchange it for a new policy on a tax-free basis if you do your homework and find that this would be beneficial.

The more you focus on insurance as a means of investing rather than paying a death benefit, the closer you come to an annuity. Annuities were created by insurance companies to enable individuals to accumulate money that they can use in their old age rather than leaving it to their survivors. Annuities are discussed in Chapter 5.

Insurance vs. Investing on Your Own

While universal life may generate a higher rate of return than whole life policies, there is still one drawback to using insurance for investment purposes: When insurance companies take the money paid in by policyholders and invest it, they buy some of the same stocks, bonds, and real estate that you could buy on your own. By investing directly in financial markets, you can pocket all the proceeds yourself (minus brokerage commissions) instead of giving a cut to an insurance company.

That's the basis for the traditional advice to "buy term and invest the difference." The advice makes sense if two conditions are met. One is that you take into account the tax-deferred status of money invested in an insurance policy. You've got to compare apples to apples and figure out if you will come out ahead without that shield from the tax collector.

The other issue is whether once you've bought term insurance, you really will invest the difference. Most people who buy term insurance don't. They take the money they've saved by not buying whole life or universal life and use it for a trip to Miami Beach, or to buy new clothes, or a used car, or whatever. The most effective response insurance salesmen have when prospects tell them they only want term insurance is, "If you save as much in the next ten years as you've saved in the last ten years, will you be satisfied?" Most people must answer no, because they have not been saving or investing. Their money has been slipping through their fingers.

Cash value life insurance has been a boon to millions of

Americans, because it has forced them to save in spite of themselves. They've had to pay their insurance premiums or lose the coverage they knew they needed; in the process they built up cash value in their policies. (In this, life insurance replicates the savings function of a home mortgage; home-owners must make their monthly payments, and thus build up equity in their homes, if they don't want to lose them.) The return on such insurance-driven savings (at least in whole life policies) has been low, but at least there have been savings.

Be honest with yourself. If you're unlikely to develop and maintain your own investment program, or you don't want the responsibility or cares of doing so, then you would be well advised to buy universal life. You and only you can decide if you're willing and able to invest on your own initiative on a relentlessly regular basis. Only you can decide whether you're willing to shoulder the risks involved in making your own investments. And you have to weigh the tax consequences of investing on your own versus letting assets accumulate on a tax-deferred basis inside an insurance account. After you've carefully thought about all that, you may very well decide you're better off buying pure insurance from an insurance company and doing your own investing.

The Need for Worst Case Scenario and Estate Planning

There was a best seller a few years ago called *When Bad Things Happen to Good People.* I don't know the answer to why bad things happen, but do I know they *can* happen, and you need to be prepared for them financially. You know you need health insurance. And you know you need life insurance. But many people don't think about prolonged periods of dis-ability. You should look into disability insurance, if you don't currently have coverage from your job. And you need to look at long-term care insurance. God forbid you have a serious stroke or other debilitating illness. It can cost $80,000 a year for nursing home care. Of course you can get it free—once your spouse has spent all of your assets paying the bills. So make sure you're insured for all manner of peril.

Make sure you also have your affairs organized so that your spouse and your family can carry on if you're out of commission. You need to identify a guardian for any minor children in case you and your spouse are seriously injured or die. You need a living will and durable power of attorney so that decisions can be made about you and about your finances when you're not able to participate in those decisions.

All this is pretty standard stuff, and any good financial advisor can tell you what to do. The problem is not finding the path, but the willingness to follow it. Some people are convinced they're immortal. Some fear the Evil Eye will hear them talking about death and disability and get ideas. Others don't trust people to make decisions about their well being. Get over it. It may pain you to envision yourself lying comatose in some hospital bed. But it should pain you even more to think about your family suffering because you're comatose and they can't get the money they need to live because you didn't get around to putting your affairs in order.

Yet another thing you have to think about is estate planning. Now you may argue that you don't have an *estate*—just a house. Estate planning is for rich people, and you've just got a home and some investments that you want to leave to your spouse and kids. But stop for a minute and add up the value of your assets—that house you bought 20 years ago may be worth a surprising sum today; the shack at the lake you bought 10 years ago has appreciated smartly since the yuppies took a liking to that particular lake; some of your investments have done nicely; and that jewelry is worth a lot more than when you bought it. So guess what, it turns out you've got an estate, and it's worth $800,000 or a million two, or more—maybe even much more.

And guess what else: There is a plan for disposing of that

estate. It's a combination of IRS regulations and state laws. Do you want this plan applied to your estate, or would you prefer to have a say on what happens to everything that you worked hard to acquire? Without proper planning, taxes can easily consume more than half of your estate. And state laws will provide a formula for distributing your assets that makes no distinctions between the kinfolk you liked and those you detested.

So you need an estate plan. The starting point is to inventory your assets. Then think about what you want to happen to them. Who do you want to reward—and not reward. You need to have a will, and you need to think carefully about what you want to accomplish with this will.

For example, in this era of blended families, maybe you love your second wife dearly, and you want to be sure she's provided for after you're gone. But if there's money left after her death, you want it to go to your kids, not hers. They're nice people, but after all you've only seen them at the holidays, whereas your kids are, well, flesh and blood. You could hope your wife will leave your money to your kids, not hers, but you could also spell out in a will precisely what you want to happen. You might set up a trust that provides your widow with a generous lifetime income, but specifies that the assets of the trust pass to your children after your wife is gone.

You not only need to spell out what you want to happen after you die, you need to develop strategies for preserving your estate while you're still alive. Estate taxes can be sizable, but there are ways of managing them. Together with your financial advisor, lawyer, accountant, or tax advisor, you might set up various kinds of trusts that minimize taxes. You should also look into "gifting." You can reduce the size of your estate—and your estate taxes—by making gifts to relatives and friends. You can give each individual up to $10,000 per year without incurring any gift tax. If you're going to give money to these people anyway, you—and they—don't have to wait until you're dead. It's tricky—you want to give away enough to reduce your estate taxes, but not so much that you'll run out of money to live on. But gifting can be a very effective estate planning tool.

And there are a host of other devices. For example, rather than sell securities to raise cash that you then give to a charity, you can give the securities directly to a charity. The charity sells the securities and ends up with the same amount of cash as if you had written a check, so it's happy. Meanwhile, you avoid incurring a capital gains tax from selling the securities, and you get a tax deduction based on the appreciated value of the securities you gave away. So you should be happy too.

While there are a lot of other things you can do, you need a good advisor in order to figure out which of those things work best for you. Just remember: You do have an estate, and if you have people in your life that you care about, then you should care about making sure you do as much as you can for them after you're gone.

CHAPTER 10

HIGH-RISK INVESTMENTS

Who Can Afford to Make Risky Investments?

Much of this chapter is about ways to lose money. Maybe you shouldn't read it. I'm sure you can think of plenty of ways to lose money on your own, without any suggestions from me, and I'm reluctant to put any new bad ideas into your head. To be sure, you won't always lose money on the high-risk investments described here, but lots of people do, including many people who didn't understand the risks they were facing and the losses they could incur. And, of course, there are some people who do quite well making risky investments. Duty demands that we cover some of the flashier investment strategies and vehicles that are mentioned from time to time in the newspapers. But note that if these investments were movies, they would be rated R, if not X: They are for grown-up investors who know something about the ways of the world. These investments can make you a lot of money—but only because they generally entail higher risks than the investments discussed elsewhere in this book.

The kind of investments we're going to talk about are often described as being best suited for "sophisticated" investors—as if there were something unsophisticated about prudent, profitable, value-based investing. ("How gauche! That man over there is drinking red wine with his fish. And that woman is buying some high-rated corporate bonds. I can't bear to watch!") In fact, so-called sophisticated investments are often the domain of speculators.

You will recall the risk/return trade-off: The greater the potential reward offered by an investment, the riskier the investment will be. Speculators deal at the far edge of that trade-off. They pursue investments that promise rich payoffs, but in return, they risk losing the entire amount they have invested. There's nothing improper or immoral about speculating. Speculators serve a legitimate economic function by assuming risks that others might not be prepared to shoulder. You can bet the ranch in the hopes of doubling your money overnight; just make sure you know (a) that you're betting the ranch and (b) that you can get along without it.

There is, of course, some risk associated with any investment. Any stock can run into trouble. Any neighborhood can hit the skids and endanger your real estate investment. And there are risks besides the prospect of losing what you invested. Investors in "absolutely safe" securities, like U.S. Treasury bonds, may find that their rate of return is less than the rate of inflation, so they risk losing some of their purchasing power.

For most investors, however, their preeminent concern is that an investment will lose money—that it will end up worth less than they invested in the first place. Investors can measure the level of risk associated with many investments with some degree of accuracy. And by being content with reasonable returns, they can saddle themselves with only modest risks. This is the kind of investment program you should have and the kind that will, over time, make you financially secure.

Speculators throw all that out the window. They want to make money fast, and they're prepared to lose their entire investment in the effort. Or at least they ought to be prepared to do so, because that's exactly what happens in the case of many speculative investments. Many of the greatest specula-tors of all time, including some who made several fortunes, died broke. The instruments and processes speculators use keep changing. Once they focused on gold claims in Cali-fornia; now it's day trading stocks via the Internet. Speculating is often a form of gambling, and many gamblers play until they lose everything. Remember that the lavish casinos in Las Vegas and Atlantic City weren't built with the winners' money.

It is often said that young people just starting out in their careers are in the best position to speculate because they have the most time to recoup any losses. Conversely, the con-ventional wisdom holds that people approaching retirement should be the most cautious with their investments because they need to husband their resources for their old age.

To this conventional wisdom, I say baloney! Consider a twenty-five-year-old accountant and her sixty-five-year-old father. The twenty-five-year-old is unlikely to have much capi-tal. She doesn't earn very much yet, and she likes to spend what she does earn. If she has saved $5,000, say, it has probably been accumulated with great difficulty. If she takes a flier with that $5,000 and loses it (which is the fate of most fliers), it may take her years to accumulate another investment stake, and she may even sour on the whole idea of investing. Moreover, the actual financial impact of what she has lost is enormous. Her $5,000, if it had been put into a more conservative investment program yielding 10 percent, would have grown to $140,512 by the time she reached her father's age. Instead, because some Bolivian gold-mining deal didn't pan out for her, she has lost not just $5,000 but also all the years of compounding and growth that $5,000 might have earned. Her speculation has been far more costly than she knew.

Her father, on the other hand, has fewer years of com-pounding to look forward to. His $5,000 loss would be a lot nearer to $5,000 than to $140,512. Besides, he has a larger income from which to get investment capital and a portfolio of other investments to ease the pain. This doesn't mean that he should gamble with money he needs for retirement; it just means that in many ways he has less to lose from a speculative investment than his daughter.

Both the persons approaching retirement and the younger person can calculate exactly how much money, if any, they can afford to speculate with. Consider a forty-three-year-old architect who would like to retire on $200,000 a year. (Actually, he'd be very happy to retire on $60,000 a year—if he were retiring tomorrow—but he has wisely built some leeway into his goal to allow for future inflation.) He figures (again allowing for inflation) that his Social Security and company pension will be worth at least $40,000 a year when he retires, so he'll need to have annual investment income by then of $160,000. He figures that he'll be able to earn 10 percent on his capital, which means he'll need to have a net worth of $1,600,000 when he retires.

That may sound like a lot of money, but our architect still has twenty-two years to go before retirement. If he can earn 10 percent a year on his investments between now and then, any money he has today will increase eightfold. (Once again, the miracle of compound interest: $1 invested in ways that yield a 10 percent per annum return will grow to $8.14 in twenty-two years.) So, to achieve his lifetime investment goal, he needs a net worth right now of $200,000. He figures his net worth by drawing up a personal balance sheet, as described in Chapter 3.

If he discovers that his net worth is $200,000 on the nose, then he must invest it prudently so that it will earn no less than 10 percent a year. For the moment, he cannot afford to speculate. If he has less than $200,000 right now, he'll have to alter his lifetime goal or accelerate his savings program. So he certainly can't afford to speculate. However, if he has more than $200,000, and more than enough to provide a little cushion beyond it, then he has money for some speculative investments. He's in a position to take some of that money and see if he can make a killing somewhere, because if it doesn't work out, he won't be killing off his long-term plan.

Everyone should be this methodical about figuring out

what they can afford to risk, but not everyone is. Some people speculate because they find prudent investing a little dull. Some speculate because they don't know that an investment they think is a sure thing is regarded by most of the world as a wild and crazy idea. And some speculate just for the fun of it. Now, I happen to think that getting rich slowly with a careful investment program is a whole lot of fun. But there's no arguing with taste.

If you can truly afford to make risky investments, like our architect friend, you have my blessing. If you truly cannot afford it but are looking for some thrills, I suggest you go ride a roller coaster at your local amusement park.

Either way, here, for the record, is a review of what I consider some high-risk investment ideas. Caveat emptor.

High-Risk Stocks

There are two ways to take big risks in stocks: by purchasing stocks that are particularly risky or by investing in perfectly reasonable stocks using risky trading strategies.

Of course, there are risks associated with all stocks. The market goes up and down, and individual stocks often go with the flow. A rising tide may lift all the boats, and a raging sea may sink many of them. As a stockholder you are an owner of a business, and that business may fall on hard times, either because the company is not well managed or because the business itself becomes obsolete.

But some stocks are inherently much more risky than others. Which ones those are is sometimes in the eye of the beholder; one person's sound investment opportunity may look to someone else like a wild flier.

Perhaps the riskiest stocks are those that are all potential. These are the shares of new companies headed by people with bright new ideas. Such companies may have no track record of earnings performance because they haven't gotten around to getting their exciting new product out into the market. But it's a dynamite concept, it really is, and as soon as all the financing is in place and the bugs are worked out of their time-travel circuit boards, the company is really going to take off. Or so they say.

A few such companies prosper over the long term. Most do not.

Hot stocks tend to cluster, decade by decade, in particular industries. In the 1950s, for example, uranium companies and then pharmaceuticals were hot. In the 1960s, the action shifted to high-technology companies and conglomerates. In the 1970s, oil stocks boomed, at least for a while. In the early 1980s, computer stocks were all the rage, and later anything having to do with biotechnology resonated with investors. In the 1990s, high-tech stocks were very popular. Any company associated with cellular telephones or the Internet would send investors into a swoon. Everybody was looking for the next Microsoft or Cisco. Companies that had no profits, no revenues—in fact, no products—nonetheless saw their share prices skyrocketing simply because they were going to do something on the Internet. More level-headed sorts kept wondering how long it would take before investors saw that some of these companies were "all hat and no cattle," as they say in Texas.

In every era, there was some sound reason underlying the popularity of certain industries. As the world changes, there is always some new industry that seems to be pointing the way toward revolutionary changes in the way we live. The problem for investors is that even if a new industry does change the world, not every company in that industry will prosper, or even survive. Pioneers often fall by the wayside. Computers have revolutionized our lives, and shares of IBM were golden for many years, but then Big Blue faltered amid the proliferation of personal computers, and its stock stalled. Apple Computer seemed to be eating IBM's lunch in the late 1980s, and its stock soared, but by the mid-1990s, it too seemed mortal.

So even if you have decided, correctly, that microwave mailboxes are about to revolutionize American life, you may not be able to pick the right microwave mailbox company to buy into. Yes, if you do pick the right one, you might make a fortune. But you'd better be prepared for the consequences of guessing wrong.

Another form of speculative stock is the "fallen angel." These are companies that have fallen on hard times and whose shares are often selling at record lows. Often these are former hot-growth issues, now battered down by investor disappointment or a generally sluggish market. Buying the shares of such companies may get you solid assets at bargain-basement prices. But you could also end up with stock certificates suitable only for lining your dresser drawers. The U.S. economic landscape is littered with companies that went into a slump and never came out of it. Maybe you're old enough to remember names like Studebaker, Braniff, or the Penn Central Railroad. If so, tell those too young to know those names that once-mighty companies can and do go bankrupt and disappear. Sometimes fallen angels never reascend.

Meanwhile, new companies are always being born. One of the wonderful things about the U.S. economy is the existence of a thriving market for venture capital. There are a vast assortment of individual and institutional investors prepared to help finance the development of new products and new companies. This has contributed to a dynamism in the U.S. economy that is envied in many other nations. It's great that there are people who are willing to take a chance on new ideas. But you probably shouldn't be one of those people, at least not until your investment program has met and exceeded your goals, giving you money to dabble in the kind of risks presented by new ideas. Until you've accumulated a sizable nest egg, stick to investing in sizable companies.

High-Risk Trading Strategies

Speculation is not only about *what* you invest in but also about *how* you invest. While some people take big risks by picking risky stocks, others incur risks by taking nice solid stocks and trading them aggressively. They're trying to beat the market in the short run, and that is sometimes akin to trying to beat a train across a railroad crossing.

One broad area of speculation consists of actively trading "cyclical" stocks. These are the shares of companies in industries like automaking and construction that tend to do very well during periods of general economic prosperity and very poorly when times are hard. The reason some industries are cyclical and some are not is fairly clear: If times are tough, you can put off buying a new car until next year, so automobile companies are cyclical. But you can't put off buying groceries until next year without getting awfully hungry, so food stocks aren't cyclical.

What is not clear is when an economic upturn is just around the corner. If the economy is depressed, and cyclical stocks are in the cellar, and you have a strong feeling that happy days are just about here again, then you can profit by buying cyclical stocks. But since you have no way of knowing for sure when the economy is about to improve, you may be buying them months or years too soon. Taking a long-term view of the cyclical movements in the economy and investing in companies that can benefit from those movements is a sound approach. But anytime you're trying to predict future events in the short run, in my view, you're taking too much risk.

Yet another high-risk strategy has been to buy shares of companies considered to be possible objects of take-over attempts. If another company or a "corporate raider" makes an offer for such a company, that party usually proposes paying substantially more than the current market price for the shares. Thus, those who own the stock stand to make a quick profit. This is especially true if the takeover bid puts the target company "in play" and other would-be acquirers bid up the price of the stock. If the acquisition doesn't go through, however, the share price may not only fall back to its original level, it may even plummet as investors see they're not going to get any takeover bonus.

You should make your investment choices on the basis of the fundamental economic strengths of a company's business. If you happen to acquire shares in a company that is put in play, and if you happen to time your sale right during the bidding process and make a bundle, consider that frosting on the cake. Don't base your investing on a search for takeover targets. There are professional investors who do this. They call it "risk arbitrage." Note the first word.

Buying on Margin

Some investors attempt to increase their profits by buying stocks on margin, which means using leverage or investing with borrowed money. If you open a margin account with a stockbroker, you can buy securities with a 50 percent down payment, and the brokerage firm will provide a loan for the other 50 percent. The securities purchased are held in the margin account as collateral. Because the collateral is always on hand, minimizing the lender's risk, margin loan rates are relatively low—generally several points lower than what banks charge for consumer loans and well below what is typically charged on credit card balances. Moreover, the interest paid on margin loans may be tax-deductible.

Margin accounts are not the only way to use leverage. You could borrow money from other sources and invest it. But the impact of leverage is the same. If you buy $10,000 worth of stock for $10,000 in cash and the value of the stock goes to $15,000, you have made 50 percent on your money (minus brokerage commissions). But if, by using a margin account, you buy $10,000 worth of stock for $5,000 and the value of the stock goes to $15,000, you have made 100 percent on your money (minus brokerage commissions and interest).

Sounds great. But leverage works both ways. Let's say you buy $10,000 worth of stock on margin, so you pay $5,000 and the value of the stock declines to $5,000. You have just lost 100 percent of your investment because you now own stock worth $5,000 and you also owe $5,000. Plus, you will be facing the discomfort of something known as a "margin call." Federal regulations require that your equity in a margin account (the value of the securities you own minus the amount you owe the broker) must always be at least 25 percent of the current market price of the securities. If you buy $10,000 worth of stock with $5,000 down and a $5,000 loan, your equity is 50 percent. But if the value of the stock drops to $6,667, your equity will be only 25 percent ($6,667 minus the $5,000 you owe equals $1,667, which is 25 percent of $6,667). At this point you must come up with some cash to repay part of your outstanding loan. If you don't have the cash, your broker will sell off some of your stock—at its depressed price—to raise the money. This can be a decidedly unhappy ending to your adventure with investing on margin, and you had better be able to afford the financial risks associated with this technique.

As is the case with so many financial tools, investing on margin is a two-edged sword that can accentuate your gains—or your losses. If you're going to use margin loans, you need to use them wisely. That means understanding the risks, making sure you have the appetite for those risks, and keeping the amount of borrowing well within your means. You should be particularly wary of using margin loans to invest in volatile sectors, such as technology, where big pricing swings can cause margin calls.

By the way, although margin loans were developed to facilitate investing, they can also be a low cost source of credit for any purpose you choose. With some brokerage accounts, you can write checks or use a debit card to gain access to money on margin. However you choose to use the funds, margin loans are still subject to margin calls. So although this is often a cheaper way to raise money than putting a purchase on your credit card or getting a personal loan from a bank, remember you are raising the risk of disrupting your investment program.

Selling Short

Selling short is a technique for trading in stocks one does not own. Typically, an investor will buy a stock in the hope that its price will go up. But short sellers do just the opposite: They sell a stock they don't own in the hope that its price will go down. What's the difference between selling stocks you don't own and selling the Brooklyn Bridge, which presumably you don't own either? Answer: There are well-established mechanisms for acquiring the stocks that you have sold short. This is the way it works:

Tom Rivera decides that the stock of International Zither Machines (IZM), currently selling for $100 a share, is overpriced and heading for a fall. I have no idea how or why Mr. Rivera made that decision. There is no way he can know for sure that the price of the stock is about to fall (unless he is dealing with illegal inside information, in which case he can expect to receive a call from the Securities and Exchange Commission). No one can *know* that the price of any stock is about to fall (or rise), since short-term movements in the stock market are highly unpredictable. That's why no prudent investment program should involve trying to guess such short-term movements. But Mr. Rivera is not involved in a prudent investment program here. He's speculating.

So, for reasons that satisfy him, Mr. Rivera has decided that the price of IZM will shortly be dropping. He goes out and sells 100 shares of the stock at the current price, $100, although he doesn't own any IZM shares. Once he has "sold short," his broker arranges to borrow 100 shares of IZM, on Mr. Rivera's behalf, from someone who does own it. The borrowed shares are delivered to the buyer, and Mr. Rivera's account is credited with $10,000 from the sale. Now all he has to do is buy 100 shares of IZM and return them to the person who lent them to him. (Until he does, he is obligated to pay the lender, out of his own pocket, any dividends paid on the borrowed stock.)

If the price of IZM goes down, as Mr. Rivera is hoping,

then returning the borrowed stock will be a pleasure. If it goes down to $80, say, he'll buy 100 shares for $8,000, hand them over, and walk away from the deal with a $2,000 profit (before commissions, of course).

If the price of IZM goes up, however, there will be no joy at Mr. Rivera's house. At $120 a share, it will cost him $12,000 to buy the shares he previously sold for $10,000. Net loss: $2,000 (plus the broker's commission on both the purchase and the previous short sale), and any dividends paid to the lender.

The life of a short seller is complicated by the fact that stocks may go up before they go down. Mr. Rivera may be absolutely right about IZM. When he "shorts" it at $100, it may indeed be on its way down to $50, but he will have a very uncomfortable time of it if the stock drops to $50 only after first going up to $150.

This will create two problems for Mr. Rivera. First, he may panic. As IZM climbs up and up, he may conclude that he was insane ever to think that it would go down and decide to cut his losses by buying it back at, say, $140, for a $4,000 loss.

Even if Mr. Rivera does not despair and remains steadfast in his conviction that IZM will fall, he may still be forced to take a loss. To guarantee that short sellers can afford to buy back the stock they have borrowed, federal regulations require that they maintain a cash balance in their brokerage account sufficient to buy back the stock at whatever its current price is. As the price of IZM goes up and up, Mr. Rivera's broker will occasionally call to ask that he deposit more cash in his account.

It's quite possible that Mr. Rivera may run out of cash before IZM hits its peak. No matter that he is still confident that IZM will fall. What if he has already sold his house and rented out his kids to keep up the balance required in his account, and IZM stock still continues to climb? If he can't come up with any more cash, then the money already in his account will automatically be used to buy back IZM—at a substantial loss for him. If the stock plummets to 0 the next day, it will be cold comfort to Mr. Rivera that he was right after all.

Derivatives

The whole nature of investment risk has been transformed by the growing popularity of derivatives. Derivatives received their name because their prices are largely derived from the price of something else. There are two main kinds of derivatives: exchange-traded contracts and over-the-counter (OTC) contracts. Exchange-traded contracts are standardized, highly regulated, and are traded on a futures or stock exchange. OTC derivatives are customized for institutional and commercial users. The kind of derivatives that most individual investors trade are exchange-traded contracts such as options, futures, and options-on-futures.

Derivatives were developed principally to suit the needs of hedgers—people who want to lock in the price of something at some future date. But the other side of hedging is speculating that the price in the future will be something other than what the hedger wants it to be. Futures and options were originally developed for the markets in agricultural commodities and precious metals, and some of these markets go back over one hundred years. In the early 1970s, futures and options concepts began to be adapted to securities, foreign exchange, and interest rate markets. Since then Wall Street rocket scientists have conjured up a wide range of these contracts.

Many long-standing forms of speculation began to look like amateur night once over-the-counter financial derivatives came along. By the early 1990s, "the D word" had become an epithet among many institutional investors. The newspapers regularly reported on major companies and large pension funds that had lost millions of dollars on fancy derivative contracts that had been used to bet on the direction of some market, a market that had perversely chosen to head in the other direction. Many participants in derivative markets forgot they were hedgers and decided to be speculators.

Individual investors can buy an assortment of derivative contracts. They're traded on major exchanges. Their prices are published in newspapers along with stock and bond prices. Major brokerage firms handle them. If you devote years of your life to the study of strips, straps, spreads, and straddles, perhaps you can make money in these markets. But most people don't. Derivatives play a useful role in major institutions with sizable staffs who spend their days analyzing and managing risks. But derivatives should carry a label that says "Don't Try This at Home." With that warning ringing in your ears, let's look at what they are and how they work.

Options on Stock

An option is the right to buy or sell a given number of shares of a specific stock at a specific price during a specific time period. An option to buy is a "call." An option to sell is a "put." This is how they work:

Joan Rivera thinks the stock of good old IZM, selling at $100 a share, is about to go up. She could buy 100 shares of IZM for $10,000. Or she could buy a "call," giving her the option of buying 100 shares of IZM at, say, $105 anytime within the next six months. If the call is quoted at $5 on the exchange where it is traded, she would pay $500 for the right to buy 100 shares at $105. (The exact price of a call will vary depending on how close the exercise price is to the current stock price, how volatile the price of that stock is, how long the option has to run, and what the general feeling is among investors regarding the prospects for the stock.)

Now assume Ms. Rivera was correct. IZM goes to $120 before the six months are up. If she had purchased the stock for $10,000, she could now sell it for $12,000, or at a 20 percent profit (minus the brokerage commissions). However, if she had purchased the $500 option instead, she would now have two choices: She could sell the option at the market price of $15, and receive $1500. This would give her a net profit of $1,000 ($1500 minus the $500 she paid for the option). That's a 200 percent return on her original $500 investment (minus, of course, brokerage commissions).

Alternatively she could exercise the option, i.e. buy the stock for $10,500, and immediately sell it for $12,000. This would also give her a net profit of $1,000 ($12,000 minus the $500 she paid for the option and the $10,500 she paid for the stock). But in order to buy the stock, she has to put up $10,500 for a few days, so she would incur a cost of capital as well as brokerage commissions, and that would result in a lower return than the 200 percent she would have earned by simply selling the option.

Imagine if Ms. Rivera had not invested $500 in a single option contract on 100 shares of IZM. What if she had taken her $10,000 and, instead of buying 100 shares of the stock, bought twenty option contracts, each giving her the right to buy 100 shares of IZM at $105. Then, if the stock went to $120, instead of making $1,000, she would have a profit of $20,000 on her $10,000 investment. That's the same 200 percent return she would have gotten buying one contract, but look at the sizable chunk of money she would have amassed buying options instead of the underlying stock. So it's clear that stock options offer far greater leverage than investors can get by purchasing the underlying stocks. Of course, on the flip side, don't lose sight of the fact that when buying options, there is always the risk of losing 100 percent of the money you invest.

What if Ms. Rivera was wrong about IZM, and the stock dropped to $80 and stayed there? If she had purchased 100 shares for $10,000, she would be looking at a $2,000 loss, but she would still have 100 shares of stock worth $8,000. If she had purchased the $500 option, however, she would only be out that $500. And if she had spent $10,000 to buy twenty contracts, she would have lost everything. The price of a stock may drop sharply, but unless the company goes out of business, the shares will be worth something and may even make a comeback. On the other hand, option contracts expire at a point in time and become truly worthless.

Options are a terrific way to make money—if you happen to be very good at predicting precisely which way particular stocks are going to move in the future. Moreover, commissions on options are high relative to the amount invested, so you have to win substantially more than you lose just to break even.

"Put" options work just the opposite of calls. You can buy an option giving you the right to sell IZM at some price lower than its current price if you expect the stock to go down. If the stock falls below the price you have selected, you can make a substantial profit. If it goes up instead, you will lose your money.

The investors who have fared the best with options have often been those who sold call options instead of buying them. If you own 100 shares of IZM at $100, you might sell a $105 call option for $500. If the stock advances above $105 before the option expires, you will have to sell it and forgo some of the run-up in its price beyond $105. But you'll still get all of the price appreciation from $100 to $105, plus the income from selling the call. If the stock doesn't go above $105, you simply pocket the $500 from selling the option. Added to the dividends paid by your stock, the money you get from selling these "covered" options can add up to a very nice rate of return on your investment.

"Warrants," by the way, are similar to call options. They are securities issued by a corporation giving the holder the right to buy a specified number of shares of the company's stock at a specified price. Warrants are often given away by corporations as "sweeteners" with bonds of less than the highest rating. Thereafter, they are bought and sold by investors just as options are.

Stock Index Options

In addition to options on individual stocks, a variety of stock index options have been created to meet the needs of people looking for a way to speculate on the general direction of the stock market. While stock options involve the right to buy or sell shares of an actual stock, stock index options provide the right to buy or sell an abstraction. There is no such thing as a "stock index" that you can hold in your hands as you can a pork belly or a share of General Motors. A stock index is just a number, derived from averaging the prices of selected actual stocks. Several kinds of stock index options are traded on various exchanges, but one of the most popular is based on the hundred blue-chip stocks that comprise an index called the Standard & Poor's 100 Stock Index.

If the S&P 100 stands at X and you think that stock prices in general are about to go up, you might buy an option to buy the index at X + 50. If the market goes up, the index will rise, and you will make money. If the market declines, you will lose. As with all options, you benefit from leverage (your actual cash investment is small compared to the amount of money you can make), and your loss will be limited to the price you have paid for the option.

Futures

While an option gives you the *right* to buy or sell something, a futures contract is an *obligation* to buy or sell something at a predetermined time and price. Futures contracts were created over one hundred years ago for a wide range of agricultural commodities and precious metals. But since the mid-1970s, futures have come to play an increasingly important role in financial markets as well.

A typical agricultural futures contract might call for the delivery of 40,000 pounds of live hogs four months from to-morrow at a price of 47.17 cents a pound. A speculator who thinks the price of hogs will rise in the next four months would buy such a contract. If hogs go up to 50 cents a pound, he will make a profit. A speculator who thinks the price of hogs will go down would sell such a contract. This is similar to the short sale of a stock; the speculator is selling hogs he does not own, hoping to buy back and liquidate the short futures position at a lower price before the last trading date.

By the way, neither the buyer nor the seller, in most cases, will ever come anywhere near an actual live hog. Before the contract's specified delivery date, they will "close out" their positions by buying or selling a contract that offsets the one they previously sold or bought and take their profit or loss. Because many of these contracts (such as hog futures and Treasury Bill futures) feature cash settlement, nobody will see a truck pull into her driveway one morning and hear the driver shout, "Hey, lady, where do you want your pigs?"

Futures contracts are available for such agricultural commodities as wheat, cattle, and coffee; energy commodities such as crude oil and natural gas; financial instruments like the Swiss franc and 10-year Treasury notes; precious metals and an array of stock indexes. Speculators in futures can make or lose large amounts of money in a very short time. Prices can be volatile and futures contracts are highly leveraged. You can buy long or sell short a futures contract by depositing a relatively small amount of cash with your broker, and a relatively small percentage change in the price of the futures contract can then double your money or wipe you out completely. Your losses can easily be greater than the initial sum deposited with your broker.

To be sure, if you are a cereal company, you belong in the futures market because you should be "hedging." You are planning to sell your Toasty Wheat Treats now and indefinitely into the future. You know that the price of wheat fluctuates, but you don't want the price of your wheat treats to fluctuate because that makes your customers nervous and also tempts them to try oatmeal. Besides, for your own peace of mind, you'd like to know what your costs will be rather than take your chances on the ups and downs of the market.

So you buy futures contracts for the delivery of wheat all through the year at a fixed price per bushel. You might buy these contracts from farmers who are hedging their own risks: They want to know right now what price they will get in six months for the wheat they planted yesterday so they can be sure they can make the payments on that new tractor they want to buy. Or you might buy these contracts from traders who are speculating that the price of wheat will go down before they have to make delivery. In either case, once you have your contracts, you no longer care what happens to the price of wheat. You have protected your position by taking advantage of the pricing opportunities offered by the futures market.

However, dear reader, please recognize that while businesses and financial institutions use futures as risk and price management tools, individuals generally trade futures with a different agenda. You have no position to protect in the futures market. You must understand that investing in futures involves substantial leverage and the risks can be substantial. If you're convinced that this marketplace is for you, then you need to do one of two things: Spend an appropriate amount of time and effort studying the workings of the futures market, or hire a professional to guide your involvement in this area. Here is when you may consider managed futures. With "managed futures," experienced professionals (called "trading advisors") manage your investments in the futures market.

In addition to commodities that grow in the ground or walk around in barnyards, futures contracts are also available on gold, silver, platinum, and other precious metals. Some people buy gold futures as a way of protecting themselves against inflation, since over the decades the price of gold has generally kept up with inflation. Buying gold futures requires less cash and entails fewer complications than buying gold itself.

Wall Street has taken the futures concept from agricultural and industrial commodities and applied it to U.S. Treasury securities, equity and economic indexes, and a variety of other financial instruments. Financial futures provide a way to hedge or speculate on changes in the direction of long-term or short-term interest rates. You can use futures to make a leveraged trade that rates will move in whatever direction your personal forecast indicates.

Similarly, futures contracts are available on foreign currencies, providing a way of speculating on the rise or fall of the Swiss franc, for example. These are very useful to people who expect to be buying or selling something in Switzerland in the next few months and want to protect their profit margin by hedging against fluctuations in exchange rates.

You may also invest in stock index futures, which work just like all other futures contracts. Futures are available on the S&P 500 Index, Dow Jones Industrial Index and many others. Unlike futures on Treasury notes or British pounds, stock index futures are "cash-settled." No actual stock certificates are delivered or received. If you hold a stock index futures position until the contract expires, the futures price will be matched to the actual cash index price. The difference between the price at which you went long or short, and the price at expiration, becomes your profit or loss. Of course, your positions may be liquidated any time the market is open; you do not have to hold the position until the final trading day.

In addition, all futures exchanges also offer options on futures. Investors can buy and sell puts and calls on futures contracts. The economics, risks and mechanics are very similar to those of equity options. The difference is that if you exercise a long put or call position, you receive a long or short position in the underlying futures contracts at your strike price.

All of these strange and wonderful instruments can do marvelous things for those who want to hedge their risks or make a large bet on their ability to accurately predict the future. Derivatives can be very useful. So can dynamite. Both need to be handled with care, if at all.

Beware of Swindles

All of the investments described so far entail substantial risks, but they are real investments that serve real economic purposes and that can provide real benefits to those who are in a position to shoulder the risks involved. But there is another category of high-risk investments, and those are simply lies. Often these lies are told over the telephone by faceless salespeople working in out-of-state "bucket shops" or "boiler rooms." They call prospect after prospect and tell a story about a great opportunity in oil leases on government land, or "strategic" metals, or fancy maneuvers in the international currency market, or some other complicated and almost plausible investment that sounds a little like something you've just been reading about in the newspapers. The salespeople on the telephone offer convincing reasons why their deals are generating fabulous payoffs, and why you have to invest right now, today, with no delay, or you will miss this unbelievable, one-of-a-kind investment opportunity of a lifetime.

Don't believe it. Don't buy. Hang up. Recognize that the voice inside you urging "Go for it!" is the voice of greed, not the voice of reason. Remember, if it sounds too good to be true, it is. There is no Santa Claus, and if there were, he wouldn't be calling you on a WATS line from Waycross, Georgia, to tell you about the outlook for titanium—a metal you may never have heard of but which is definitely about to face shortages so severe that its price will skyrocket.

Scoundrels have always been attracted to the investment world. Wall Street has, if anything, been a place where reputable firms have operated on high principles. People regularly commit millions of dollars on the telephone because they know that reputable people at reputable firms regard their word as their bond. But at the fringes of finance, there has never been a shortage of crooks. It is, after all, a world that deals in pieces of paper; there is no heavy lifting, no bulky products to move around, just people trying to persuade you to send them money in return for pieces of paper.

Sharpies used to get you to part with your money in face-to-face encounters. The telephone made it possible for swindlers to widen their purview considerably, and besides, you could run nationwide scams out of boiler rooms located in pleasant climates. Technology marches on, and today there are regular reports of questionable investment tips and dubious deals being put forward by unidentifiable people via investment chat sites on the Internet. In the late 1990s, *The*

New Yorker ran a cartoon showing two dogs in front of a computer. One tells the other, "On the Internet, no one knows I'm a dog." On the Internet, you don't know if that sure-fire advice being proffered in a chat room is coming from a market wizard, a misguided naïf, or an outright swindler. You don't know the reliability of the source nor the reliability of his or her facts.

Whatever the communications medium, there are always some people attempting to sell blue sky and hot air. That's why investors should always take care to learn whom they're dealing with as well as what they're buying.

CHAPTER 11

MANAGING YOUR PORTFOLIO

Getting Richer

I know a man who moves a lot. This is a great inconvenience, but his career requires it. And it does offer him one useful opportunity. Every time he moves, all of his belongings end up piled in the middle of his new living room. Moreover, reorganizing his desk brings him face-to-face with records of financial assets not kept around the house. Gazing at the accumulation of his worldly goods, he can make a quick calculation: Is the pile bigger than it was the last time he moved? Is he moving, asset-wise, in the right direction?

Accumulating capital, building your net worth, advancing toward your goal of financial serenity. These are things that can only be accomplished over the course of many years. You can't do these things with one quick killing. It requires planning, discipline, and time. As particular investments come and go, and milestones in your life roll by, there will inevitably be times when you lose sight of the big picture. But the main focus should be your progress. Are you getting richer?

You should be, if you've followed the general principles we have discussed so far and if you have put your money into some of the specific investment vehicles we've described. But there is more to a successful investment program than making sure you put your money in the right places and avoid the wrong places. Investments do not take care of themselves, even when you have the help of an able broker. You must prune them and nurture them and give them regular attention. In short, you don't just pick investments, you also have to manage them. So here are some rules and suggestions for the care and feeding of a lifetime investment program.

Diversification by Type, or Asset Allocation

First of all, your investment program should have a varied diet. Obviously, you would be foolish to put all your money into the stock, or bonds, of one company. That would leave you vulnerable to being wiped out if that company encountered hard times. If all your money is invested in Worldwide Widgets, what happens if it's discovered that widgets cause cancer? Or the federal government suddenly imposes a 55-mile-per-hour speed limit on widgets. Or the Japanese find a way to make widgets out of seawater? Or an earthquake opens up the earth behind the headquarters of Worldwide Widget and swallows up the main production facility? You've got to be diversified to spread out your risks.

It's not quite so obvious, but it would also be foolish to concentrate your money in a single type of asset. If, for example, your portfolio consists entirely of fixed-income investments— bonds, certificates of deposit, and other types of "lending" investments that pay predetermined rates of interest—you are highly vulnerable should soaring inflation rates ever take hold. You would have to watch helplessly as the real value of your net worth declines. If you own only common stocks, on the other hand, you are protected from the worst effects of inflation, but you are vulnerable to the effects of a recession or a major downturn in the market.

A well-balanced portfolio should include both fixed-income

investments and common stocks. And neither component of your program should consist of a single security. You should own different stocks (or a stock mutual fund) and several different bonds (or a bond mutual fund or unit investment trust). Your portfolio might also include other kinds of investments, such as shares in real estate investment trusts, and you might also choose to own some "hard assets," such as gold or silver.

By keeping your eggs in several baskets, you achieve a couple of things: You have a shot at participating in whatever market happens to be turning in the best performance. Conversely, you avoid the risk of the big losses you might have suffered if all your money was in a market or an investment that did badly. Sure, your returns will suffer if you only have a portion of your assets in the stock that took off, but that's better than having all your assets in the stock that tanked. As we've seen, it's difficult to climb out of a hole and recoup not only what you lost but the compounded earnings you would have had without that loss. Any opportunities that you've missed are offset by the impact of diversification: Because you have some investments in markets that zigged when others zagged, you'll keep having positive returns that will benefit from the magic of compounding.

When you're thinking about diversification, by the way, make sure you include all of your assets. Besides your investment portfolio, you may have a 401(k) plan at work and money held in a trust account for your children. Each may be diversified on its own, but make sure that they don't overlap too much. Some people buy the same stock for all accounts and end up with their investments too heavily concentrated in a single stock or a single kind of investment.

To visualize where you stand, it may be useful to draw a bar graph representing your assets. Assign a different color to each type of asset—fixed-income, common stocks, real estate, gold, collectibles, whatever. You might be surprised to see a single color dominating the chart. You may not have realized how heavily weighted your portfolio is toward real estate if your main asset is your house, or how it tilts toward fixed-income investments if most of your money is in bank accounts, money market funds, and bonds (all of which are fixed-income investments). If a single color dominates your bar graph, you must work toward making it a rainbow.

Major institutional investors engage in formal asset allocation studies to decide how they want to divide up their investments, and they reexamine these studies at regular intervals. You need to do the same thing. You need to make sure your eggs are not only in the right baskets but also in the right number of different baskets.

Diversification over Time

Just as it's important to diversify by type of investment, it's also important to achieve some diversification in the timing of your investments. This frequently overlooked principle applies to all investments.

In the case of bonds and other fixed income investments, you don't want to buy them all at once and you don't want them to all mature at the same time. The reason is the volatility of interest rates. If you buy all at once, you may lock in high rates—or you may lock yourself into the lowest rates in years. Since you can't forecast where rates are going, its useful to invest in fixed-income instruments over a period of time, so the interest rates you get average out. Similarly, you want diversification in maturities. That way, you always have some investments maturing and you have access to cash if you need it. Moreover, just as you don't want to take the risk of making your original investments when interest rates are at low levels, you don't want to have to reinvest all of your money at low rates either.

Unless or until you can forecast interest rates with absolute precision, you're better off having an investment program that is diversified over time so you're constantly investing at current interest rates. On average, you'll be much better off this way than hoping that you'll be able to plunge in at the highest rates.

Issues of timing are equally important for stocks. Suppose you have reached, as you inevitably should, a decision to invest a portion of your net worth in stocks. You and your broker have selected a list of stocks for your portfolio. Wisely, you are not planning on putting all your money into a single company. Instead, you've chosen half a dozen stocks, all in different industries. You've picked companies that you have good reason to believe are well positioned to create real wealth over the long term. They're competently managed companies, and they're not the Fad of the Month (which could mean that they were ludicrously overpriced). You're ready to buy. You show up at your broker's office with check in hand. Take my money, you say. It's burning a hole in my pocket. Call up Wall Street and get me in.

Slow down.

Think for a minute. You know how the market is. It goes up and down. Up a bit, then down a bit, then down some more. Then up, then down. Then down. Then up. Odds are, in the long run it is going up. It always has. Odds are, in the long run the stocks you have selected will go up too. But the long road up will be obscured by countless detours up and down. It always is.

At any given moment, it is impossible to know whether the market is "high" or "low." You can only guess where it stands in the complex cycles through which it endlessly gyrates. Some of the reasons for the daily ups and downs may seem apparent. A bill to cut taxes is approved by a congressional committee. Or interest rates move down. But other market movements seem totally inexplicable. When you hear a market commentator say, "Investors nervous about the Middle East brought the market down today," or "The market rose as Wall Street anticipated a drop in widget prices," there's no way you can know those things are absolutely, positively true. Maybe it was the Middle East, but maybe it was concern about unemployment, or maybe it was sunspots. If people knew precisely why the market moved the way it did on any particular day, they would be billionaires.

So, the market bounces up and down unpredictably, and there you stand on the sidelines, check in hand, ready to dive in. Since you can't know if the market's next bounce is up or down, the prudent thing to do is not to jump in all at once. If you're planning on investing $25,000 in eight stocks— about $3,000 per stock—buy three of the stocks today and put the remaining $16,000 back in your money market fund. A couple of months from now, take out another $9,000 and buy three more stocks. Wait another couple of months, and then buy the rest.

Don't be upset if the market moves in the meantime, as it inevitably will. If the market moves up before you have completed your purchases, then you'll pay more for some of your stocks than you would have if you had bought them all at once. But so what? The stocks you bought first have gone up. You're already ahead. Congratulations. If the market goes down, don't be alarmed. You've picked your stocks for good reasons, and even a major market drop does not necessarily alter the fundamental value of the companies. If their stock prices have fallen, so much the better. When you buy them, you're getting a bargain.

The real benefit of this diversification over time is that you buy into the market at something approaching an average price and avoid the risk of making your entire investment at what turns out to be a temporary peak.

When this approach is transformed into a formal, ongoing schedule of investing, it's called "dollar-cost-averaging." This eminently sensible way to invest calls for investing the same amount of money at regular intervals in the same stocks. Say, for example, that you have $3,600 a year to invest. You decide to dollar-cost-average, so on the first of every month you will put $300 into the stock market, including $100 into General Bones, which you are convinced has excellent long-term prospects.

Let's see what happens with that stock (and for the sake of

argument, let's forget about commissions). On January 1, General Bones is selling for $10, so you get 10 shares for your $100. But then the stock sinks to $5 a share, so your next $100 gets you 20 shares. Then the bone market explodes, and by March 1 your stock is at $15. For your $100 you get 6.7 shares. By April 1, the bone hysteria is over and the stock is back at $10, right where it began. You buy 10 more shares.

How do you stand? The stock sank five points below its starting point, then rose five points above its starting point, then went back to where it began. You're even, right?

Wrong. You're ahead. Figure it out. Your total investment was $400. You have purchased 46.7 shares. You can sell them today (with the stock back at $10) for $467. Good going.

What happened here is testimony both to your strategy and to your strength of will. When General Bones sank to $5, you did not panic and bail out. You kept buying, and because the price was down, you got more shares for your $100. (Conversely, when the price was up, you got fewer shares for your $100.) Dollar-cost-averaging is a reliable strategy that gives you significant protection from the ups and downs of the market. In fact, those movements can make you money.

In real life, where there are brokerage commissions, the focus on dollar-cost-averaging may have to be tempered a bit because transaction costs may be relatively high if you make a number of small transactions; you may be better off from a commissions point of view if you blend your buying and selling into a smaller number of trades. Thus, you may need to invest larger sums, or trade quarterly instead of monthly. But you should always keep the principles and benefits of dollar-cost-averaging in mind when you're planning to put money into an investment. And these principles don't just apply to direct investments in securities; they're equally applicable to investing in mutual funds. One way to keep on the dollar-cost-averaging track is to arrange for money to be automatically transferred from your checking account to an investment account each month.

If a company you invest in has a Dividend Reinvestment Plan (DRIP), by the way, you can use that to help with your dollar-cost-averaging. Companies which have DRIP let stockholders use the dividends the company pays on their shares to buy additional shares of company stock at the closing price on a predetermined date. These plans typically let you buy fractions of shares, so it doesn't matter if your dividends are only a portion of the price of a share. And many of these plans also let you purchase substantial amounts of additional shares at the same time. DRIP plans not only help an investor take advantage of dollar-cost-averaging, they also make it possible to buy stock without any brokerage commissions.

The Virtues of Patience

Of course, you will not be buying General Bones or anything else if you have not yet begun to convert some of your income into capital dollars. The necessity not to spend all that you earn underlies everything else in this book, and it has either sunk in by now or you are wasting your time by continuing to read.

Once you have accumulated the capital to buy some stocks and you have purchased a small portfolio diversified by company, industry, and time, what then? How do you know when to buy more and, more to the point, when to sell?

The ideal strategy, of course, is to buy low and sell high. Buy stocks only at their all-time lows and sell them at their all-time highs. This is a lovely strategy, but you would have to be clairvoyant to get it right. No mere mortal can know when these highs and lows are occurring. You may be convinced a stock's price has reached a turning point, but tomorrow may see a lower low or a higher high. Until you learn to see into the future, you had better have a different plan.

Our basic rule is to sit. In contrast to other fields of endeavor, on Wall Street it is frequently true that more money is made by sitting than by doing something. Certainly many of the largest American fortunes have been made by people who acquire assets and hold them for a long time. The only way I have ever made money in the stock market is by buying a good stock and holding on to it. This strategy can also work for you.

It will probably test your patience, however. And it may test other aspects of your personality as well. Many of you who have the capability and desire to get rich slowly are undoubtedly driven by the American work ethic. You can't believe that any worthwhile activity you engage in can produce good results if you devote less than 110 percent of your time and energy to it. This may be true of many human activities, but it can be counterproductive in investing.

Successful investing requires that you identify good value by finding companies that are creating wealth, and that you then associate yourself, through your capital, with these companies. Then you should sit and hold this stock over the years while your judgment is vindicated. Don't assume that by doing nothing you're "doing nothing" and getting paid for it. In investing, sitting tight is often as hard a job as frenetic buying and selling.

The American work ethic will play a role in your success—indirectly. The people running the companies you have selected should be consumed by it—but you should not. While they work day and night to make your companies successful, you must resist the urge to think too much about the stocks and to trade them, selling them when the market is high and buying them back when the market is low. If you start playing those games, you will inevitably lose. You will end up selling too soon and buying too late. You will be outsmarted at least 50 percent of the time by the people from whom you are buying and selling. And even if you win half the time, you will still lose because of brokerage commissions and other transaction costs.

So relax. Take it easy. Buy and hold.

The hardest part of this will be disciplining yourself to ignore the "noise" of market movements. The market is always going up and down, but most of those movements have nothing to do with the value of the stocks you have selected. It will not be easy for you to remember this. When your stocks go down, you will be convinced you have made terrible misjudgments in buying them. (Occasionally this will be true; usually it will not.) When your stocks go up, you may decide you are a stock market genius and be emboldened to start "playing the market," which, I assure you, will be a costly mistake. The market goes up and the market goes down. Don't take it personally.

Weeding the Garden

So our basic rule is buy and hold. But—and you're expecting a "but," aren't you?—that doesn't mean you should be pigheaded. Sometimes you will make a mistake. And sometimes there will be fundamental changes in the economy or the marketplace or the management of one of your companies which will require you to react. I once knew a man who had a lot of gilt-edged ferryboat company bonds, and then somebody built a bridge.

When you are managing your portfolio, your tactic should be to keep the winners and weed out the losers, always bearing in mind that not every stock that goes down is a loser. All stock prices dip from time to time, usually in tandem with the rest of the market. This "noise" is a different phenomenon from the slide of a company that has developed a serious problem.

The tactic of keeping winners and selling losers, while it may seem obvious, is, in fact, precisely the opposite of what most people do. When a stock goes up, they sell it, take their profit, tell everybody how smart they are, and look for something else to buy. When a stock goes down, they hold on for dear life, waiting for it to rise back to its former level, although there is no good reason why it should. Inevitably, by selling their winners and holding their losers, such people end up in the unhappy position of owning a portfolio of stocks that are all losers.

These loser-holders often operate on the theory that "it's not a loss until I take it." Or they hold their positions out of simple lethargy, believing that it's wisest to leave poor enough alone. Or they feel loyal to a stock, as if it were a human being. "General Widget Corporation has been good to me," they say, looking back to past successes. But take my word for it, General Widget Corporation doesn't even know you. Don't fall in love with a stock. It will not return the favor. When you have made a mistake, and it is clear that you own a turkey, sell it. There's no point in postponing the day of reckoning. A loss is a loss, before you sell it. So sell it now, take your tax loss, and put the money into something better.

There are also times when you should sell winners, despite the general rule to hold them. Sometimes you will be fortunate enough to pick an unpopular, undervalued stock that a year or two later becomes the fad of the moment and gets driven up to an inflated price that has little to do with the company's underlying value. Sell. Sometimes you own a stock that becomes the object of a bidding war in a takeover attempt. Sell. In general, sell if circumstances make a stock overpriced. If there has been a temporary bounce in the price of a stock, capitalize on it. Take the money that you expected to earn over the next two years but is being offered today and reinvest it. But don't sell if the stock is only rising in price to or near the value that attracted you to the stock in the first place. The best may be yet to come.

It turns out there are no "one-decision" investments. You and your broker should think carefully about what you want to invest in, and once you've made the investment, alas, you and your broker have to keep thinking about it: Is this still the right investment, or is there another alternative that has become more attractive?

Measuring Performance

As time goes by, you will want to monitor the performance of the investments you own (and thus, indirectly,
the performance of the broker who recommended them).
To be meaningful, these evaluations must be more complicated than simply noting which investments are up and
which are down.

This is particularly true in the case of stocks. Stock performance should be measured in comparison with market
trends. Yes, your stocks are down 5 percent, but if the market
as a whole is down 15 percent, then they (and your broker)
are performing heroically. If, on the other hand, your stocks
are up 20 percent while the market is up 30 percent, wipe that
grin off your face. You are not doing as well as you should be.

A major complication in evaluating the performance of a
stock is the difficulty of separating "real" price movement
from the distracting background of market "noise." Here is a
graph of the price movement of a stock (movement that will
typically coincide more or less with the movement of the
market as a whole):

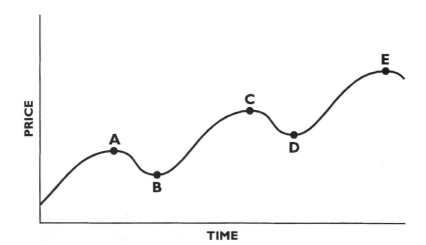

If you bought the stock at point A and evaluate its performance at point B, you will be very unhappy. (You will probably blame your broker for your unhappiness and fire him or her.) If you bought at point B and evaluate at point C, you will be ecstatic. (You will probably credit yourself entirely for your success and congratulate your broker only for being wise enough to select you as a client.) In both cases, your conclusions will be wrong.

The best measure of the stock's performance is to compare peak to peak (point A to point C to point E) or trough to trough (point B to point D). Measured that way, this stock is doing nicely. The only way to take this measurement, however, is from a long-term perspective. You never know at any given moment whether you are at a peak or a trough or somewhere in between. Only months or years later can you look back and see the picture clearly. This is one more reason to hold the stocks you buy, barring fundamental changes in their underlying value. Historically, most stocks have moved up from market cycle to market cycle. If you choose your stocks carefully and diversify sufficiently to compensate for the mistakes you will make anyway, then your portfolio, on average, should move up too.

More and more investors have at least some of their assets invested in mutual funds, and those also require measurement and evaluation. The good news is that their results are calculated for you: You can look in the annual report sent to you by the mutual fund and see what return the fund has offered for the last quarter, the past year, and often for the previous five- and ten-year periods. The bad news is that you need to give some thought to the meaning of these results. As in the case of stocks, you should assess your mutual funds in relative rather than absolute terms: Being up 20 percent last year may sound great unless the market as a whole was up much more than that.

There are two other things to note: First of all, as in the case of stocks, you should evaluate mutual funds over an extended period. Anything less than a couple of years is meaningless. You need to look at three years of performance figures at a minimum, and maybe more. As with stocks, you want to look from peak to peak, across an entire market cycle, to see how the fund did. Short-term results give too much weight to accidents—such as individual investment selections that happen to have done very well or very badly. If you look over a longer period of time, the role of happenstance is reduced and you get a more accurate picture of how good a job the mutual fund manager is doing in selecting and managing investments for you.

In addition to looking at results over a significant period of time, you also need to examine a mutual fund's results in comparison with its peers—other mutual funds with the same investment objective as your fund. The thousands of mutual funds now available generally have fairly specific investment objectives: Some are seeking rapid growth, some seek to balance growth and income, some focus only on international stocks, some invest only in value stocks. At any point in time, the specific markets or market segments that your fund invests in may be doing better or worse than other parts of the investment world. Sometimes growth stocks, for example, do better than value stocks, and sometimes they don't. When they aren't doing as well, that doesn't mean there's anything wrong with investing in a growth stock fund, but it does mean you shouldn't expect the growth stock fund manager to be achieving results as good as a value stock fund.

Thus, you should look at your mutual fund results over the long term, and when you look at those results, you should not only compare them to overall stock market indexes, like the Standard & Poor's 500 Stock Index, but you should also compare your fund's results to those of similar funds. This kind of information is often reported in articles in the *Wall Street Journal* or in your local newspaper. It's also available in articles in magazines that focus on personal finance, and there are services, like Lipper Analytical Services and Morningstar, that compile this information.

If you have hired an investment manager, you need to

follow the same process in evaluating his or her performance as you would in evaluating a mutual fund: Look long term and compare the results not only to the overall market but also to others who have the same investment style or philosophy as your manager.

Everybody is entitled to a bad year or two. But if your investments are trailing the market year after year for periods of more than three or four years, then it's time to think about a change. If you've entrusted your funds to a mutual fund or investment manager, it may be time for some new blood. If you're picking your own investments, it's a little harder to fire the manager. But you do need to rethink what you're doing.

When Ed Koch was mayor of New York City, he was known for asking his constituents, "How'm I doing?" You should be asking yourself the same question about your investments. And if the answer isn't positive after a while, it's time to do things differently.

Moving Toward Your Goal

The most important evaluations you will make as the years go by will be those that measure your progress, or lack thereof, toward your ultimate goal.

As I've said before, you must define a goal for yourself. Maybe you want to have $500,000 by age sixty-two, to have $800,000 by age sixty-eight, to have $1.98 by next Tuesday— whatever. But without a definite goal, you will have no idea if you are reaching it.

Once your goal is established, you can calculate what combination of savings and investment growth you must achieve to reach it. Buy a pad of graph paper (or a graphics/spreadsheet program for your personal computer). Spend some time plotting where various rates of savings and compound interest will lead you from your present situation. Plot where you must be every six months for the next ten years on the road to your goal. You will quickly see exactly how easy or how hard it is going to be to get to your destination.

Your task will be hopeless if your goals are unreasonable. Remember, you can't count on finding $10 stocks that will go to $15 in six months. Aiming for too high a rate of return will lead you to take speculative risks that will almost certainly wreck your entire program. To repeat some basic principles: Seek a reasonable rate of return. Start investing early. Let years of compound interest work for you.

You should calculate your net worth once or twice a year to see if you are meeting the targets on your graph. See how much of your income has been converted into capital, and how fast your capital is growing. If you're falling behind, you must rethink your investments, or increase your savings, or both.

It's not unreasonable for you to plan on becoming a millionaire. There are several million millionaires in the United States, but there's always room for one more. Remember, if you invest $64 a week starting at age thirty, if you achieve a 10 percent annual return, your money will grow to $1 million by age sixty-five.

Achieving that goal, or a comparable one, will bring you to a state of financial serenity. Monitoring your progress along the way, seeing your investments succeed and your assets pile up, watching your net worth grow from year to year, will spread that serenity throughout your entire life.

Is the effort worth it? As the saying goes, "It's just as easy to fall in love with a rich girl as a poor one." Let me paraphrase that: For most Americans, it's almost as easy to go through life getting richer as staying poor. And it feels a whole lot better.

CHAPTER 12

THE ECONOMIC
FACTS OF LIFE

The Individual and the Economy

Judging from the headlines, the situation is hopeless. The dollar is up, and American workers are losing their jobs because of cheap imports. The dollar is down, and people are losing confidence in the American economy. Inflation is up, so your real income is declining. Inflation is down, so you'll never sell your house for much more than you paid for it. Interest rates are up, so businesses can't afford to expand. Interest rates are down, so your savings aren't growing very fast.

What's a person to do?

News reports about the economy seem to find negative consequences in every development, and they often portray the individual as a helpless victim buffeted by endless economic storms. It's not surprising that many people glance at the financial pages of their newspapers with resignation, sighing at news they barely understand. All that's clear to them is that whatever the news is, it almost certainly isn't going to do them any good.

In fact, the news is not as bad as it seems. How could it be?

The U.S. economy rolls on in complex and unpredictable ways, as it always has and always will. Most of the moves in its erratic course produce both losers and winners.

The only sure thing about the economy is that it will change, and that those caught on the wrong side of the change will be losers—at least until the next change in the opposite direction. Of course, some changes are fundamental. It doesn't appear that the American steel industry, for example, is about to recover its former prosperity. For the indefinite future, it will not be a good idea for young people to count on careers in the mills. But the decline of American steel is part of a global realignment of economic activity. Starting in the 1970s, a substantial number of American manufacturing jobs seemed to be disappearing. Employment dropped in such industries as steel, textiles, and garment manufacturing.

Some of those jobs were moved to low-wage countries, particularly in Asia. Some of those jobs simply ceased to exist because of technological advances in manufacturing techniques. Ultimately, these jobs were replaced by new jobs in service industries or in fields created by new technology. Many of those jobs didn't even exist when the steel mills were last going strong. Meanwhile, new kinds of manufacturing techniques were taking hold in the U.S., and the nation's economy was becoming much more competitive than it had been a few years earlier. Despite the loss of many manufacturing jobs, the U.S. economy has created millions of new jobs in the service sector. Today, there are far fewer steel workers in Pittsburgh than there were in 1970, but there are hundreds of thousands of people in Silicon Valley making vast sums at jobs that didn't exist in 1990, much less 1970. The world changes, and it is a sign of maturity, both personal and national, to accept major changes and to adapt to them.

Much of the financial news deals with changes that are short term—the dollar is up, the dollar is down, stocks closed higher, stocks closed lower—and you don't have to sell your house because of them. If you keep your head and try to understand what's happening—and what's not—you can weather these periodic economic crises, and maybe even profit from some of them.

The Specter of Inflation

Take inflation.

Everybody knows that during the late 1970s and early 1980s America endured a period of high inflation. What Americans went through in those years certainly did not compare with the German hyperinflation of the early 1920s, when prices rose 1 trillion percent in 22 months, until it cost $100 billion marks to mail a letter. Nor did our 1970s experience compare with the inflation Americans suffered following the Revolutionary War, when the purchasing power of the Continental dollar dropped to one thousandth of its original value. Nor did the American experience in the 1970s compare with the inflation that raged in Argentina, Brazil, and many other countries during much of the 1970s and 1980s.

Nevertheless, what happened to most Americans in the 1970s came as a shock, largely because we had no recent experience with inflation. During most of the 1950s and early 1960s, the annual inflation rate was less than two percent, and sometimes less than 1 percent. Some people seriously suggested that inflation might be gone forever.

But inflation returned, as it always does. At first, Americans didn't mind it very much. People's salaries were going up, the values of their homes were going up, and business profits were going up. It made people feel prosperous to have more money to spend, even if, because of rising prices, they could buy less with it.

Once people caught on to what was happening, however, a vicious circle set in. It's one thing to get an unexpected 10 percent pay raise and then notice, gee whiz, that prices just happen to have gone up 10 percent too. It's another thing when you start to expect prices to go up 10 percent a year.

Then, when you're negotiating for your next raise, you're going to demand (quite reasonably) that your salary go up not just 10 percent, because that would only keep you even, but, say, 15 percent. But if your employer gives you and your coworkers 15 percent raises, then even if he hadn't previously planned on it, the prices of the products he manufactures are likely to be going up 15 percent next year.

In an inflationary cycle, this pattern begins to spread through the economy. Labor contracts begin to contain cost-of-living escalators, guaranteeing that wages will go up when prices rise. And prices rise, so wages go up, which raises manufacturing costs, which causes prices to go up, which causes wages to go up. And so on.

This pattern of inflation as a self-fulfilling prophecy took hold in the United States in the late 1970s. What had cost $1 to buy in 1970 cost $2.47 in 1980. This was not bad news for everybody. People who had bought $30,000 homes in 1965 with 6 percent mortgages found that their houses were now worth $100,000 and the monthly payments they had worried so much about being able to afford back in 1965 now looked like bus fare.

The banks and savings and loan associations collecting those piddling little mortgage payments were not so pleased, however. Neither were people on pensions and other fixed incomes that were not "indexed" to go up when inflation rose. Imagine a couple who retired about 1959. At the time, they congratulated themselves for having shrewdly managed their financial affairs so that they were guaranteed a retirement income of $800 a month, for life. This looked pretty good in 1959. By 1979, they were desperate. These people had made their financial arrangements during a prolonged period of low inflation, and they made the mistake of assuming that what had been would continue to be.

It came as little solace to our newly impoverished couple and people like them, but during the 1970s, a new generation of investors made a similar mistake—only in the opposite direction. Because they were living during a prolonged period of inflation, they assumed that would continue. So they bet on it, and they lost.

Whether investors win or lose during an inflationary period has a great deal to do with interest rates. If you put your money in a savings account, and the bank pays you 5.5 percent a year for the use of your money, that's all well and good—unless the rate of inflation is more than 5.5 percent. If it is, then the value of your money (that is, the amount of goods you can buy with it) will actually be decreasing while it is sitting in your savings account earning interest.

While the interest rates on simple savings accounts are fixed, the rates on more sophisticated investments are in a constant state of flux. The United States Treasury, for example, sells three-month Treasury bills every Monday at Federal Reserve Banks. Those who buy these bills are making short-term loans to the United States government.

How does the government set the interest rate on these loans? It doesn't. The bills are sold in an auction system. Investors bid on them, and the bills go to those who are willing to accept the lowest rate of return on that particular Monday. What that rate is depends on several factors, one of the most important of which is what investors expect to happen to the rate of inflation. If inflation is currently running at 10 percent, nobody is going to bid to buy a Treasury bill paying 8 percent. If inflation is running at 5 percent, then 8 percent is just about right.

Seasoned investors do not focus on the "nominal" interest rate of an investment; they keep their eye on the "real" interest rate, which is the difference between the nominal (or stated) interest rate on an investment and the current rate of inflation. If your money is in a bank account paying 5.5 percent interest and the inflation rate is 5.5 percent, then your nominal interest rate is 5.5 percent, but your real interest rate is 5.5 minus 5.5, or zero. That means the purchasing power of your money is not increasing at all.

Historically, investors have expected a real rate of return of about 3 or 4 percent on safe investments. Short-term Treasury bills are about the safest investment around, so they generally end up selling for only 3 to 4 percent above the current inflation rate.

During the inflationary 1970s, inexperienced investors gradually caught on that their money wasn't doing them much good in savings accounts. In 1979, for example, while banks were paying 5.5 percent on savings, the cost of living went up 13 percent. So the real interest rate on a savings account that year was a negative 7.5 percent. At that rate, thanks to the wonders of compound interest, any money you had in a savings account would have rapidly shrunk toward nothing.

Fortunately for the average investor, changes in the banking laws and innovations in financial services during the 1970s opened up new methods of saving that offered higher rates of return. Money market funds and certificates of deposit, paying substantially higher rates of interest than savings accounts, were made available to people of moderate means, and many took advantage of them. For the first time, Mr. and Mrs. North America could get access to the same financial instruments as large institutions.

Some individuals looked for even more profitable ways of staying ahead of inflation. They began to buy *things*. It was the price of things, after all, that was going up year after year, while the value of money was decreasing. So people began to buy all kinds of things—gold, rare stamps, Oriental rugs, antique cars, antique Barbie dolls, you name it. The value of precious metals and collectibles soared during this period.

The most popular thing of all during the heart of the inflation years was real estate. Land and housing prices seemed to be going up without end. You couldn't possibly lose money buying real estate. Buy something today, sell it next year, and make a pile of money.

Real estate investments were especially profitable because of leverage. If you bought a $100,000 condominium for $100,000 cash and sold it a year later for $120,000 you made 20 percent on your money. Not bad. But what if you bought a $100,000 condominium for $20,000 down and took out a mortgage to pay for the rest? If you sold the unit a year later for $120,000, you would have made $20,000 on an actual cash investment of only $20,000. So you have made 100 percent on your money (less carrying charges). This is leverage in action. It made a lot of money for a lot of people.

In fact, the people who made out best during the inflationary period were those who owned a lot of property, owed a lot of money, and had very little cash.

Not every borrower got into the game that early, however. In fact, a lot of people got into the game at exactly the wrong time. They borrowed money to buy property after interest rates had risen to take inflation into account. But they shrugged that off. So what if the interest rate on their loans was high? The real estate inflation rate was even higher. They could always sell out in a couple of years and make enough profit on their properties to cover the high cost of the loan. Right?

These late-arriving borrowers failed to take into account the one sure thing about the economy: that it will inevitably change. After a decade of high inflation, and several fruitless attempts to slow it down, the Reagan administration and the Federal Reserve Board took measures that finally succeeded. They were harsh—the cure for inflation required a deep recession and high unemployment—but they worked. (The Reaganites also got a lucky break; oil prices fell.) By 1982, the inflation rate had dipped to less than 4 percent.

When the switch in the trend came, it took interest rates a while to adjust. It always does, because investors tend to assume that what has been happening in the economy for the last few years will continue to happen. Thus, when inflation first took off in the 1970s, interest rates lagged behind. The real interest rate on Treasury securities, usually 3 to 4 percent, was actually negative for periods immediately following the sharpest inflation peaks of the decade. During this period, the Treasury (and other borrowers) got a very good deal, but lenders got burned.

When inflation dipped in the early 1980s, the tables turned.

Investors didn't believe they could trust the new low-inflation trend to continue, so interest rates stayed high. For a while, the real interest rate on Treasury securities was 8 percent. Lenders did very well for themselves. But borrowers were in plenty of trouble.

By the end of 1984, home mortgage foreclosures had reached their highest point in more than a decade. Tens of thousands of families found they couldn't afford their high-interest mortgage payments. A few years before, they could have resolved the situation by selling their houses for a tidy profit, paying off their mortgages, and buying smaller houses. But real estate values had leveled off. Many people couldn't sell their houses at a profit. So they lost them.

Real estate speculators across the country faced the same trouble, because leverage works both ways. Just as it enables investors to make 100 percent on their money in a single year when property values are racing upward, it permits them to lose 100 percent of their money in a single year when property values come down. During the great boom of the 1970s, speculators had their cake—and they ate it.

By the mid 1990s, inflation had been dead for a number of years, and once again there were learned debates about whether it had been killed off forever. The Federal Reserve Board continued to see signs of inflation lurking in various corners, but the man and woman in the street no longer assumed that prices were going up every year or that wages were destined to rise as well. The financial institutions that were so eager to shift to variable rates found that those rates could follow the consumer price index down as well as up. And those who had variable rate mortgages foisted on them in the 1980s were patting themselves on the back in the 1990s for being so clever in arranging low-cost home financing.

The moral of the story is that inflation comes and it goes. Don't assume it, but don't assume it's gone either. You need to be protected in case inflation surges. Putting all of your money into fixed-income investments, no matter how safe they are, is still a highly dangerous game. You may safely collect all of your interest and principal and not have enough money to meet your needs. But putting all of your money into commodities and gold and hard assets or real estate isn't wise because if there is no inflation, these may appreciate only modestly, and meanwhile you'll be missing all the dividends, interest, and capital appreciation that financial investments could have generated for you.

The message embedded in every chapter has been that you don't have a crystal ball, and it's time to say it again: You can't predict the future, so you should arrange your affairs so that you can deal with various economic and financial environments. Don't assume that tomorrow will be just like today. There's a saying on Wall Street: Trees don't grow to the sky. Things keep going up until they don't, and other things keep falling in price until they stop. You can't be perfectly hedged against all eventualities. But you shouldn't assume that you know for sure where the financial world is heading.

The Upward Trend

In the end, there is not much an individual can do about most of the cycles the economy goes through. You should always keep an eye on interest rates, of course, and consider moving some of your investment dollars from stocks to bonds when interest rates go up. You might also want to buy real property at the start of an inflationary period. Of course, that's a little like saying you should buy stocks when they're going to go up. The tricky part here is figuring out exactly when an inflationary period is starting. If you make your move from cash to hard assets late—as many people invariably do—you may find that prices have already been jacked up to what will turn out to be their peaks, and you'll be stuck with some extremely expensive rare stamps.

Since the odds are that you won't be able to predict the start of the next period of high inflation, it's a good idea to keep some portion of your net worth in the kind of assets that will rise with inflation. In investing, diversification is always a sound strategy.

The most important thing to keep in mind is that in the long run, the cycles even out and the economy moves ahead. What goes around comes around. Wealth is still being created in this country, despite the cyclical ups and downs and all the momentary panics. In the short run, things may look shaky, but in the long run, things tend to advance. And we live our lives in the long run.

It doesn't profit most individuals to worry too much about this year's economic or financial crisis. And it doesn't profit a prudent investor to be overly concerned with the short term. To be sure, you have to keep a close eye on markets if you're hoping to sell some stock in order to pay for your son's college tuition next semester. But overall, when investing you should probably assume that the country is going to continue to prosper, as it has prospered, over the long run, for more than two hundred years. If that trend comes to an end, and the country enters a terminal Great Depression, you'll lose everything. But then you would have lost everything no matter what you did.

I refuse to believe that America is on its last legs. I know all about the short-term uncertainties and the gloomy pundits who see the specter of 1929 around every corner. I know the litany of concerns about foreign competition and stalled productivity and diminished entrepreneurship. In the case of most of those laments, I've seen them come, and I've seen them go. The fundamentals are strong. The spirit of enterprise constantly renews itself.

And there is a happy symmetry between individual investments and national economic health. When entrepreneurs create products and companies, they not only enrich themselves, they also provide jobs for thousands of people and rewards for thousands of investors as well. Similarly, through the act of investing, individuals make it possible for American industry to grow by turning over their hard-earned money to link their capital to American industry. These investors profit as industry profits, but then the American economy requires savings and investment to finance its development and expansion. Without the dollars individuals put into stocks and bonds and other securities, America would grind to a halt. Those investment dollars finance the American future. When that future arrives, it will continue to reward those who have invested in it. Think of it: Your efforts to achieve financial serenity help the nation advance its aggregate economic serenity. When you build your nest egg, you build up the country's economy. And vice versa. It's a beautiful thought, isn't it?

INDEX